SOUL&
SPIRIT

A Glimpse into Biblical Psychology

Together with
Papers on "Soul-force" versus "Spirit-force"
from *The Overcomer*

by

JESSIE PENN-LEWIS

CHRISTIAN • LITERATURE • CRUSADE
Fort Washington, Pennsylvania 19034

CHRISTIAN LITERATURE CRUSADE
U.S.A.
P.O. Box 1449, Fort Washington, PA 19034

GREAT BRITAIN
51 The Dean, Alresford, Hants. SO24 9BJ

AUSTRALIA
P.O. Box 419M, Manunda, QLD 4879

NEW ZEALAND
10 MacArthur Street, Feilding

ISBN 0-87508-953-4

Copyright © 1999
Christian Literature Crusade
Fort Washington, PA

Originally published by
Overcomer Literature Trust
England

First American edition 1992
This printing 2000

Cover photo credit: SuperStock/Gregory Martin

Scripture quotations are generally from the
American Standard Version of 1901.

Printed in the United States of America

CONTENTS

APPENDIX

"Soul-force" Versus "Spirit-force"

CHAPTER 1

SOUL AND SPIRIT

(HEBREWS 4:12)

THE ignorance of Christians concerning the distinction between "soul" and "spirit" is very general and is a primary cause of the lack of full growth in the spiritual life in many devoted and earnest believers. G. H. Pember points out as one cause of this ignorance the popular phraseology "soul and body," which has caused a deficiency in the English language. He also says that although we have the nouns "spirit" and "soul"—which are too often treated as synonyms—we have no *adjective* from the latter. The consequence is that the omission of such an adjective has nearly concealed man's tripartite nature in most versions of the English Bible, where the Greek word which signifies "pertaining to the soul" is sometimes rendered "natural" and sometimes "sensual" (1 Corinthians 2:14, James 3:15, Jude 19).

Of course Greek scholars know well the different words in the original which stand for spirit—*pneuma;* soul—*psuche;* flesh—*sarx.* To most Christians these distinctions are veiled. The result is that they are unable to discriminate in experience between things that differ and yet which vitally belong to their peace. The need for this knowledge is of more than academic importance, for the fallen archangel Satan, with his superhuman wisdom, knows the make-up of human beings. Posing as an angel of light, he brings to bear all the power of the knowledge which he possesses. He can counterfeit the working of the Holy Spirit and CREATE IN THE REALM OF THE SOUL such perfect imitations of the pure life of the Spirit of God indwelling the man's spirit that the most earnest Christians are liable to be deceived. It is therefore necessary that the teaching of the Scripture upon the distinction between soul and spirit should be made as clear as possible from the Word of God so that even the youngest believer can understand those distinctions.

The writer is not attempting to meet the need of those who are able to go directly to the Greek New Testament and read it for themselves. Rather, it is to assist those who must have help here as they earnestly

seek the aid of the Spirit of God to enable
them to grasp the truth and to receive spiritual understanding of spiritual facts set
forth in the Scripture as necessary for their
growth in life and godliness. Let the reader,
then, pause at this point, and in an act of
faith take the promise of John 14:26, *"The
Holy Spirit . . . shall teach you all things . . ."*
and John 16:13, *"He will guide you into all
truth . . ."* with confidence that the Spirit of
God will fulfill His office to the teachable
child of God. The Holy Spirit is able to
teach the believer in *experience* the distinction between soul and spirit without his
ever knowing the truth intellectually. And
vice versa, the scholar may see clearly the
difference as expressed in the Greek but
not know at all what the words mean *experientially—i.e.,* he may hold the truth in
mental instead of spiritual power. Then it
is but the letter of the Word without the
spirit. Therefore, the believer who has been
taught personally by the Holy Spirit "the
dividing of soul and spirit" before apprehending the distinction with his intellect is
better able to understand and "rightly divide the word of truth" than the reader of
the Greek who is untaught of God. For
back of the words in the Scriptures there
are spiritual verities which cannot be understood by the natural man—*i.e.,* the "pertaining to the soul" man (lit. 1 Corinthians

2:14)—and can only be known by revelation.*

But first as to the missing adjective! G. H. Pember says that an attempt is being made to use the Greek word "psychic" for expressing in English the adjective for soul. The word is, however, too Greek, so to speak, to commend itself for general use. In connection with James 3:15, Pember uses the word "soulish," and this seems more nearly to express what is needed. Stockmayer also uses this same word—"soul-ish"—to signify that which pertains to the soul, for he says in reference to 1 Corinthians 2:14, "the Greek text has it, the 'soulman,' or 'soulish-man.' As 'spiritual' is the adjective of spirit, so is 'soulish' the adjective of soul." The word "soulish" therefore might well be generally accepted by English readers as the missing adjective, which will enable us to speak of the "soulish" Christian as well as the "spiritual" (1 Corinthians 3:1) and the "carnal" (fleshy) Christian, and the meaning be understood. For this purpose it will be so used in the present treatise, even though no dictionary lists the word.

As to the distinction between soul and spirit, Gall points out that not only in the English language is the distinction made, but in every classic language from Hebrew

---

*See 1 Corinthians 2:10–12, *Conybeare and Howson* translation.

downward. Yet, in the English New Testament only two passages bring out the distinction clearly: Hebrews 4:12—*"Dividing soul and spirit"*—and 1 Thessalonians 5:23—*"Sanctify you . . . spirit and soul and body."* These two, however, are sufficient for the English reader to see that man *is* tripartite, and not only soul and body.

THE SOUL AND ITS FUNCTIONS

Two questions must be asked here: "What is the 'soul' as distinct from the 'spirit'?" And "What are their respective functions?" Before we turn to the Scriptures, here are some quotations from other writers which will help us to discover what the apostle means by "the dividing of soul and spirit," and thus more clearly understand how "spirit and soul and body" can be sanctified and preserved blameless unto the coming of the Lord.

Tertullian, one of the Church Fathers who wrote in the early centuries of the Christian era, calls the "flesh"—or physical being—"the body of the soul," and the soul "the vessel of the spirit." The soul stands between the spirit and the body, for "direct communication between spirit and flesh is impossible; their intercourse can be carried on only by means of a medium"*—the

---

*G. H. Pember in *Earth's Earliest Ages.*

soul being that medium.

The "soul was the meeting place, the point of union between body and spirit," also writes Dr. Andrew Murray. "Through the body, man—the living soul (Genesis 2:7)—stood related to the external world of sense; through the spirit he stood related to the spiritual world."

Pember explains the function of each very clearly when he says, "The body we may term the *sense*-consciousness; the soul the *self*-consciousness; and the spirit the *God*-consciousness." Again he says, the body "gives us the use of the five senses"; and the soul, "the intellect which aids us in the present state of existence, and the emotions which proceed from the senses," while the spirit is the highest part which "came directly from God, and by which alone we apprehend and worship Him."

Dr. Andrew Murray agrees with this when he writes that the gifts with which the soul was endowed when man became a "living soul" were those of "consciousness, self-determination, or mind and will"; and these were to be but the "mold or vessel" into which the life of the spirit was to be received. Dr. Murray also says: "The spirit is the seat of our God-consciousness; the soul of our self-consciousness; the body of our world-consciousness. In the spirit, God dwells; in the soul, self; in the body, sense."*

Again, Pember writes concerning the creation of man and how the tripartite being was formed: "God first molded the senseless frame, and then breathed into it the 'breath of lives' (Genesis 2:7. The original is in the plural)." This "may refer to the fact that the inbreathing of God produced a two-fold life—*sensual* (in the meaning of pertaining to the senses) and *spiritual*. . . ."

He adds, in a footnote, that possibly the meaning of the use of the plural in the "breath of lives" is that "the inbreathing of God became the spirit, and *at the same time by its action upon the body, produced the soul.*"

Briefly, we see that all these writers practically define the "soul" as the seat of the personality, consisting of the will and the intellect or mind; a personal entity standing between the "spirit" with its openness to the spiritual world, and the "body"—open to the outer world of nature and sense; the soul having the power of choice as to which world shall dominate or control the entire man.

For instance, when Adam walked in the garden of Eden, the spirit breathed into him by God dominated his "soul"—*i.e.*, intellect, mind, will—and *through the vessel of the "soul"* shone out in, and through, the

---

*Dr. Andrew Murray in *The Spirit of Christ*.

earthly tabernacle of clay—the body—making it radiant with light, impervious to cold and heat, able perfectly to fulfill the object of its creation.

THE FALL OF MAN

But—alas, that a "but" has to be written—man fell, and after a time the result was seen as described by the Lord Himself in His words, "Every imagination of the thoughts of his heart was only evil continually" (Genesis 6:5). The "Fall" apparently began in the intellectual department of the soul, for it is said that Eve saw that "the tree was to be desired to *make one wise*" (Genesis 3:6, *ASV*). The appeal of the Serpent was not made to the vessel of clay or the outer man, for the body was then perfectly dominated by the spirit; but it was directed to the intellect and understanding of man and was based on a lawful desire to advance in knowledge and power in the unseen realm of another world. "Ye shall be *as God*," said the Serpent, not "Ye shall be *as the beasts*," created by God! The temptation was KNOWLEDGE, the very knowledge which probably God meant to give in due season—but which, grasped before its time and out of God's will, involved disobedience.

The words of the Apostle Paul in 1 Corinthians 1:19 are therefore very significant in connection with this aspect of the Fall, for the "word of the cross" is said by the apostle to be the power of God to "*destroy the wisdom of the wise.*" Since sin entered through the avenue of the intellect, salvation comes by a cross which destroys the fallen "wisdom" by the very acceptance of its message, for the preaching of "Christ crucified" is to the wisdom of men "foolishness" (1 Corinthians 1:18–25). Thus God, in His wisdom, provides salvation in a way which deals with the cause by which the Fall came about! Therefore Paul writes, "If any man thinketh that he is WISE among you, . . . let him become a FOOL, that he may become wise. For the WISDOM OF THIS WORLD IS FOOLISHNESS WITH GOD (1 Corinthians 3:18–19, *ASV*).

Eve, moreover, fell through yielding to the very temptation which had caused the fall of Satan himself, for he had said "I will be like the Most High . . ." (Isaiah 14:13–14). The tempter knew how to attract Eve; he suggested to her something *higher than she possessed,* for she was limited by a body made of dust, but had a soul capable of appreciating knowledge and growth, through the higher part of the tripartite being.

The full effect of the downfall we do not see until years afterward, when the record of the condition of the race shows that the road down was rapid, for the "wisdom" which gave knowledge of good and evil in the Garden of Eden reached its ultimate in due course in a complete sinking into flesh, so that the part of man's tripartite nature which he had in common with the animal creation obtained the upper hand. Then it was that God looked down upon the fallen race and said, "My Spirit shall not abide in man . . . for in their going astray they are *flesh*" (Genesis 6:3, *ASV* margin). And so it is that not only has "death reigned" over the fallen race of Adam, but every human being born in the likeness of the first Adam is "of the earth, earthy" (1 Corinthians 15:47), and is dominated by the flesh instead of the spirit. The soul, which is the personality of "himself" (see Luke 9:23), is a slave of the flesh and the earthly life instead of being a handmaid of the spirit.

Thus the condition of the unregenerate man is now (1) his human spirit is severed from God, fallen and alienated from His life (Ephesians 4:18), "without God," separate from Christ (Ephesians 2:12), and incapable of fellowship with Him; (2) the soul—intellect, mind, will, self-consciousness—*may* rule over the body, or (3) the body in its desires and appetites may be enslaving and dominating the soul. But while the human spirit is thus "dead" to God, and in darkness, it remains as full of activity as mind or body. In some instances the spirit part of the unregenerate man may be so large in its capacity that even in its dark condition it dominates the soul and body. Then the man may be said to be "spiritual," in the sense of possessing more spirit than others who are mainly soulish or fleshly. These are the ones who seek intercourse with the spirit-world apart from the Holy Spirit of God and become "mediums," capable of exercising occult powers, such as clairvoyance, etc., bestowed upon them by satanic means. For *unless the human spirit of a man is regenerated and indwelt by the Holy Spirit of God,* it is in accord with the fallen spirits of Satan and governed by the prince of the power of the air, the spirit that now worketh in the children of disobedience (Ephesians 2:2–3).

We see, therefore, that the fallen spirit of man—bereft of God at the Fall—sank down, so to speak, into the vessel of the soul; and the soul again sank down into the fleshly body, under what Paul the Apostle calls "the power of the flesh," so that in the unconverted "the soul, manifested sometimes in intellectuality, sometimes in sensuality, often in both, reigns over them with undisputed sway. This is what Jude wishes to set forth in his 19th verse, which should be rendered, 'These be they who separate, men *governed by soul,* not having spirit . . .' "*

Fausset very clearly brings this out in his commentary on this passage, for he

*Pember.

writes, "In the three-fold division of man's being . . . the due state in God's design is that 'the spirit' . . . should be first, and should rule the soul, which stands inter-mediate between body and spirit, but in the . . . natural man, *the spirit is sunk into subserviency to the animal-soul*, which is earthly in its motives and aims. The 'car-nal' sink somewhat lower, for in these the flesh, the lowest element, . . . reigns para-mount."*

In regeneration it is the darkened and fallen "spirit of man which is quickened again and renewed."† This is the meaning of the Lord's words to the "master of Is-rael," to whom He said, in spite of all that he knew in intellectual religious knowledge, "Ye must be born FROM ABOVE" (John 3:3, also margin v. 7), and later on to His dis-ciples, "It is the Spirit that quickeneth; the *flesh* profiteth nothing" (John 6:63).

The way that the new life from above reaches the fallen spirit of man is shown in the Lord's words: "The Spirit *breatheth* where [He] will, . . . so is every one that is born of the Spirit" (John 3:8, *ASV* margin); and, in John 3:14–16, the cause of the Spirit of God quickening the spirit into new

---

*Fausset's Commentary on Jude 19.
†Dr. Andrew Murray's notes in Appendix to *The Spirit of Christ*.

life is given as the death of the God-Man upon the cross in the place of the sinner, "that whosoever believeth *into* [lit. Greek] Him should not perish, but have eternal life."

The Cross and the Fall exactly and perfectly correspond—the one as the remedy for the other. First, by the death of the Saviour on the cross the *sin* had to be put away and the way made possible for the Holy God to pardon the sinner. Second, the sinner must be given a way of escape from the bondage of soul and body into which he had fallen. The tripartite nature of man could then be again adjusted, with the spirit once more in domination and the body acting merely as the outward and material vessel—the instrument of the spirit through the soul.

This way of escape is made clear in many parts of Scripture where we are shown the death of the sinner *with the Saviour*. Its mode of application for deliverance we shall see later on, as we consider the full meaning of the Cross.

CHAPTER 2

THE CARNAL CHRISTIAN

"And I, brethren, could not speak unto you as unto spiritual, but as unto carnal, as unto babes in Christ" (1 Corinthians 3:1, ASV).

LET us repeat at this point that the soul is the seat of the self-consciousness (the personality, the will, the intellect), and stands between the spirit—the seat of the God-consciousness—and the body—the seat of the sense, or world-consciousness. Gall says that the "soul" derives its life, or animating power, from either the spirit (the higher part) or the animal (the lower part). In Latin, the word for "soul" is *anima*—the animating principle of the body.

In the converted man—*i.e.*, one who has had his spirit regenerated, or quickened into life, by the Spirit of God communicating life to the fallen spirit—the soul is dominated either from beneath, *by the animal-life*, or from above, *by the spirit-life*. It may be said, therefore, that there are three classes of Christians,* and these three classes of believers are clearly referred to in the Scriptures as

(1) *The spiritual man*—dominated by the Spirit of God, indwelling and energizing his renewed human spirit.

(2) *The soulish man*—dominated by the soul, *i.e.*, by the intellect or emotions.

(3) *The carnal man*—dominated by the flesh, in fleshly habits or desires, *i.e.*, "the power of the flesh."

The Greek word used in 1 Corinthians 3:1 is not *psuche*—soul, but *sarkikos*—fleshly, the adjective of the word in Romans 8:7, where it is written that "the carnal [*sarx*] mind is enmity against God." It is not said that the *"psuche,"* or soulish life, is enmity to God, but the *fleshly mind*. It is true that the natural or "soulish" man cannot receive, or understand, the things of the Spirit (1 Corinthians 2:14), but he is not said to be in enmity simply because he is soulish! *"And I [i.e.*, as the natural man—

---

*There are only two classes of men: saved and unsaved, regenerate and unregenerate; but different classes of believers, described according to growth and knowledge in the life in God.

'man of soul,' Greek—cannot *receive*, so I
also] could not *speak* unto you the deep
things of God, as I would to the spiritual;
but I was compelled to speak to you as I
would to *men of flesh*,"* wrote Paul, in effect, to the Corinthians, for although truly
regenerate—and "in Christ"—yet they were
so dominated by the *flesh* that he could
only describe them as still "carnal" or
fleshly. This was proven by the manifestation of the works of the flesh in jealousy
and strife, for he writes to the Galatians:
"the works of the flesh are manifest, which
are these: fornication, uncleanness, lascivi-
ousness, idolatry, sorcery, *enmities, strife,*
jealousies, wraths, factions, divisions, par-
ties, envyings, drunkenness, revellings, and
such like" (Galatians 5:19–21, *ASV*). Any of
these manifestations seen in a believer
mark the workings, in some degree, of the
"*sarkikos*" or fleshly life, passing out
through the avenues of the soul, or personality, in jealousy or strife, etc. Such a one
is not even a "soulish" man—*i.e.*, merely
"natural"—but a man walking "after the
flesh," even though his spirit may be re-
vived and quickened into life. Those who
are thus walking "in the flesh" cannot
please God.

The apostle's description of these

---

*Fausset.

Corinthian believers as being "carnal" or "fleshly," and yet "babes in Christ," shows clearly that "babes in Christ" are generally under the domination of the flesh—or "in the flesh"—at the initial stage of their spiritual life. In their regeneration they are truly "in Christ"—*i.e.*, vitally quickened with His life and planted into Him by His Spirit, as it is written in John 3:16, "that whosoever believeth into Him may have everlasting life" (Greek); but these "babes in Christ," vitally in Him by a living faith, have not yet apprehended all that the cross severs them from by their being baptized into His death on the cross and quickened by His life.

It appears from the apostle's language that he blames these Corinthians for being still "babes," for the babe-stage ought not to be of very long duration (Hebrews 5:11–14). The regeneration of the spirit—which comes through the inbreathing of the Spirit of life from God, upon a person's simple faith in the atoning sacrifice of the Son of God on the cross in his behalf—should be quickly followed by the apprehension of *the death of the sinner with the Saviour* (Romans 6:1–13), which brings about the deliverance from life after the "flesh"—which the Corinthian Christians had manifestly not yet known. The marks of the carnal Christian—babes in Christ—the apostle sketches very clearly, and by these marks every believer of the present time can judge for himself whether he, too, is "yet carnal." This leads us to consider at this point:

THE DELIVERANCE OF THE CROSS

"They that are of Christ Jesus have cruci-fied the flesh" (Galatians 5:24, *ASV*). These are the words with which the apostle ends his description of the "works of the flesh" in his letter to the Galatians, as he contrasts the "fruit of the Spirit" which the "spiritual" man—the man in whom the spirit, indwelt by the Holy Spirit, rules—should bring forth in his life.

The "babes in Christ" who are "yet car-nal" need a fuller grasp of the meaning of the cross; for in the purpose of God the death of Christ meant that the "old man" was crucified with Him, so that "they that are of Christ *have crucified the flesh*" with all its affections and desires. The same cross that was revealed to the unregener-ate man as the place where sin was atoned for, and his burden of sin removed by the blood of the Lamb, is the place where the "carnal" Christian—who may be a "babe" in Christ, even though regenerate for many years—must obtain deliverance from the domination of the flesh, so that he may walk after the spirit and not "after the flesh," and thus in due season become "spiritual" and a full-grown man in Christ.

ROMANS 6 IS THE MAGNA CHARTA OF LIBERTY THROUGH THE CROSS OF CHRIST, which the babe in Christ needs to know, for it most clearly sets forth the basis of deliverance, to which only a brief reference is made in Galatians 5:24 and other passages.

Only by an appropriation of death with Christ, with the putting to death of the "doings" of the body (Romans 8:13, *ASV* margin; Colossians 3:5) can the believer live and walk and act in and by the Spirit, thus becoming a spiritual man. "When we were 'in the flesh,' the passions of sin . . . wrought in our members to bring forth fruit unto death," wrote Paul to the Romans, "but now we have been discharged from the law, *having died . . .*" (Romans 7:5–6, *ASV* margin).

"In the likeness of sinful flesh" (Romans 8:3), the pure and holy Son of God hung upon the tree, an "offering for sin," and because He died for sin, and *to sin* in the place of the sinner, God thus has condemned forever a life of "sin in the flesh" in all who are truly united to His Son. The believer lives "in the flesh" (2 Corinthians 10:3) it is true, in that he is still in his physical body, but once he sees God's own Son in the "likeness of sinful flesh" hanging upon the tree, and knows that in Him he died to sin, from that hour he lives "in the flesh" (Galatians 2:20) as far as the physical body is concerned but he does not WALK any longer "after the flesh"—that is, according to the demands and desires of his body—but "after the spirit"—that is, according to his renewed spirit indwelt by the Spirit of God. (*Cf.* Romans 8:5–6.)

Based upon the work of the Son of God on the cross of Calvary, in which the sinner for whom He died was identified with the Substitute who died for him, the redeemed and regenerate believer is called to "reckon" or account himself "dead to sin," because "our old man was crucified with Him." The Holy Spirit of God dwelling in his spirit can then carry out to its ultimate issue the divine purpose that the "body of sin"—*i.e.*, the whole continent of sin in the whole of fallen man—may be "destroyed" or "abolished,"* as the man on his part steadily and faithfully "refuses to let sin reign" (Romans 6:6, 12–14). It is as the "babe in Christ" knows this that the "flesh" ceases to dominate and have control; he rises in spirit into real union with the Ascended Lord— *alive* unto God in Christ Jesus.

The "babe in Christ" who grasps this now knows the fuller meaning of being "alive unto God"; and walking after the spirit, and by the Spirit, he ceases to fulfill the desires of the flesh, and henceforth gives

---

*See next page.

his spirit, indwelt by the Spirit of God, the domination of his entire being. It does not mean that he may not again lapse into the walk "after the flesh." But as long as he gives his mind to "the things of the Spirit," and reckons himself continually "dead indeed unto sin," he "by the Spirit" steadfastly "makes to die" the "doings of the body" (Romans 8:13, *ASV* margin) and walks in newness of life.

---

*"The word *destroyed* in the KJV is rendered *'done away'* by Alford, and *'annulled'* by Darby. In Romans 3:3, it is translated *'make without effect'*; in Romans 3:31, *'make void'*; in Romans 4:14, *'made of none effect'*; in Romans 7:2, *'loosed'*; in Romans 7:6, *'delivered.'* Whatever its best translation in Romans 6:6, it is plain that it signifies that 'the body of sin' is to CEASE TO HAVE ANY POWER TO BRING THE BELIEVER INTO BONDAGE TO SIN . . ."—W.R.N.

The root word means "to leave unemployed, to make barren, void, useless." Therefore the actual "abolishing" of the "body of sin"—which includes practically all that we receive by nature in the first Adam—can only reach its ultimate experientially when the "body of our humiliation" is "conformed to the body of His glory" at the coming of the Lord from heaven (Philippians 3:21).

CHAPTER 3

THE "MAN OF SOUL"

"The 'natural' man ['man of soul'] receiveth not the things of the Spirit of God . . . because they are spiritually discerned" (1 Corinthians 2:14, lit.).

CHRISTIANS who have arrived at the stage of knowledge of the cross where they cease to walk "after the flesh" think that they are now "spiritual" believers, entirely renewed and led by the Spirit of God. But then comes the most important lesson, says Dr. Andrew Murray—the lesson concerning the danger of the *"inordinate activity of the soul,* with its power of mind and will"—the "greatest danger" which "the Church, or individual, has to dread."*

The believer who has been quickened in spirit is born of the Spirit, and the Spirit of God dwells in his spirit. He has had the

---

*Dr. Andrew Murray. Note in Appendix to *The Spirit of Christ*.

revelation of the cross which has shown him the way of victory over the life after the flesh, and he now walks in newness of life and in victory over sin as manifested in the "works of the flesh." But at this stage the question must be asked: What about the "soul"—the man himself in his personality, his intellectual or emotional activities? *Which power is animating the actions* of the man himself apart from the "works of the flesh"? Is he animated and governed by (1) the spirit life which comes from above— from the Risen Lord as the Last Adam, the Life-giving Spirit, or (2) by the life which comes from the lower realm—the fallen life of the first Adam?

We have already pointed out the error of the prevailing idea that when the believer has comprehended his death with Christ to SIN, and ceases to walk habitually "after the flesh," he becomes a "spiritual man" and is "entirely sanctified"! Merely to be delivered from the domination of the flesh, or carnal life, does not mean that he ceases to be "soulish"—or *ceases to walk after the life of nature;* for the "death to sin" and crucifixion of the "flesh" is only one stage of the work of the Spirit of God to be done in the redeemed man. He may cease to be *"sarkikos"*—or fleshly, and still be *psychical*— or "soulish," *i.e.*, living in the realm of the soul instead of the spirit, or God-conscious sphere.

To understand this clearly, we must consider what are the evidences of the Christian being *"soulish,"* when he ceases to be "carnal" or living "after the flesh."

The soul, we have seen, includes intellect and emotions, as well as the central personality which makes it the seat of one's self-consciousness. The believer may be entirely freed from the manifest "works of the flesh," as described in Galatians 5:19–21, while his intellect and emotions are still moved by the *"psuche"* or *"animal-soul"* life—*i.e.*, they are not yet renewed and fully animated by the Holy Spirit working through the regenerated human spirit. The soulish Christian is therefore one whose intellect and emotions are still governed by the first-Adam life and not by the Life-giving Spirit of Christ (*cf.* 1 Corinthians 15:45) who brings the intellect and emotions under full control as the believer walks after the spirit. Yes, the Holy Spirit may dwell in his spirit and enable him to "make to die the deeds of the body" while his intellect and emotions are still "soulish."

If we take, for instance, the question of the intellectual life, a passage in the Epistle of James very clearly shows the distinction between the heavenly and the soulish—or natural—wisdom. The apostle writes that the wisdom which is *not* "from above" is (1) earthly, (2) soulish (*psychikos:* the *ASV*

margin gives "natural" or "animal"—*i.e.,*
pertaining to the soul), (3) demoniacal (*ASV*
margin), and produces jealousy and fac-
tion, division and partisanship. On the
other hand, the wisdom which *is* "from
above"—that is, from the Spirit of God
dwelling in the spirit of man—is character-
ized by purity, peaceableness, gentleness,
mercy and good fruits, and so partakes of
the divine character that it is *"without partiality"* (James 3:15–17). The pure heavenly
wisdom is without any element of the
soulish life—the place of *self*-conscious-
ness, *self*-opinions, and *self*-views—and
therefore causes peace instead of strife and
envy. The third statement, of the soulish
wisdom being *"demoniacal,"* will be dealt
with in another connection.

In the light of the passage in James, how
clearly we can see the condition of the
Church of God and why it has split up into
sections and "parties." Often, alas, the
"works of the *flesh*" in jealousy and strife
are the causes of "factions, divisions, parties" (Galatians 5:19–20, *ASV*) in the as-
semblies of God's professing people. But
there is another cause of disunion in the
professing Church where the *soulish intellect* is the separating factor. *We see soulish
"wisdom" so handling divine truths* as to
facilitate the world of demons in fostering
division among the followers of Christ.

Pember remarks that "the intellect is not merely fallible, but the *most dangerous of all gifts,* unless it be guided by the Spirit of God." And yet among Christians it is relied upon for the grasping of divine truth, and for the understanding of spiritual verities, while the Scripture declares that the "soulish" man—and this includes even the believer insofar as he is "soulish"—cannot "receive" the things of the Spirit, because they can be only *spiritually* discerned.

Again, it is the *soulish element in teachers and professors of holiness* which is often the cause of separation and disunion. There may be, it is true, love in the heart to those who "differ." But the "differences" divide nevertheless, because the demoniacal powers, able to work upon the soulish element in the believer, always emphasize or exaggerate the differences in "views of truth" instead of magnifying the points of union, even driving eager believers to "fight" for their view of "truth" under the name of "witnessing for God." Devoted believers, alas, think they are seeking the blessing of others, while unknowingly doing the same as the Pharisees, in compassing "sea and land to make one proselyte . . ." (Matthew 23:15).

It is also the soulish element in Christians which insists upon the minute correspondence of others to its "views of truth," and "tithe mint and anise and cummin" in *words* while leaving "undone the weightier matters of the law"—which in the gospel dispensation is the law of Christ, and places love and the unity of the Spirit between believers as the condition of their growth into "unity of the faith" (Ephesians 4:3, 13).

In brief, the soul-life, influenced by evil supernatural powers, is the main cause of divisions and separations among the professing, and even the true, children of God. "These be they who separate, men *governed by soul* . . ." writes Jude (verse 19). "Separate themselves" is the *KJV* and "make separations" the *ASV* text. "Arrogant setting up of themselves, as having greater sanctity; and a wisdom and peculiar doctrine, distinct from others, is implied," writes Fausset in his commentary. Fausset also translates the word "sensual" in this passage as literally *"animal-souled."*

"Separate *themselves*" as "having greater sanctity" is always a mark of the soulish life, for the Lord Jesus said, "Blessed are ye, when men shall hate you, and when *they* shall separate you . . . for the Son of man's sake" (Luke 6:22). The Apostle Paul also said in answer to a question about separation, "Let each man abide in that calling wherein he is called," and therein "abide with God." God Himself will "separate" those who walk in light and those who abide in darkness *by His presence as the Light,* and often the one who elects to walk in the "darkness" will either cast out the one abiding in the light, or himself be brought into the light. Men can be "governed by soul" even when they have the Holy Spirit, and these soulish ones always "separate themselves" and "make separations," proving that in *some degree* they are "soulish" and not "spiritual."

The other department of the soul-life is the emotional, which *proceeds from the senses of the body.* Here again a Christian may be swayed by the soulish and think it all "spiritual." Pember says that a "knowledge of Biblical psychology dissipates the idea that any holy spiritual influence can be set in motion by *appeals to the senses.*" Yet the reaching of the spirit through the *senses* is the purpose of many church services, and even mission meetings where the gospel is proclaimed. Pember's words on this subject are illuminating. He says, "Splendid buildings, gorgeous vestments, and picturesque rites for the eye, with sweet odors for the scent, and ravishing music for the ear, although they may bewitch one's consciousness with the most agreeable sensations, can *penetrate only as far as the soul* . . . [yet] our spirit . . . does not receive its impressions from the senses, but *only from spirit*. . . ."* He points out, also, that the order of our being from God's point of view is *spirit,* soul, body, because "God's influence commences in *the spirit,* then lays hold of the emotions and the intellect, and lastly begins to curb the body." From the standpoint of Satan the order is reversed. We have (1) earthly, (2) soulish, (3) demoniacal,† because Satan's influence *enters by the clay made body;* then seizes upon the soul; and, whenever possible, gains entrance to the spirit.

How solemn are the facts herein set forth. How clearly they show why the churches are filled with nominal worshipers of Christ, who show *no marks of a true Christian life within them!* How sad it is that the very presence of these worshipers shows that within the spirit they have an unconscious cry after God, which in thousands of cases is never satisfied. For either their soul-life in its intellectual department alone is met by intellectual, soulish presentation of the letter of the truth, or their sense-life is gratified by soothing music, and the calming influences of the hour of quiet, without their being led into real worship of God *in spirit* and in truth, which alone is acceptable to Him.

---

*Pember's *Earth's Earliest Ages.*
†James 3:15.

Are all these influences to be depreciated? God forbid. But they will not *save* the "soul"! They may, and do, prepare the way by bringing the person within reach of the truth which is read from the Scriptures, if not preached in the pulpit, and all these outer things that make for righteousness have their value and place.

But—and this is the serious danger—influences that PENETRATE ONLY TO THE SOUL ✓ and do not reach the spirit in regenerating power are deceptive. They give the person a "*form* of godliness without the power" and bring the spiritual religion of Jesus Christ down to the level of heathen philosophies and cults. Hence "religious" men who are merely "men of soul" place the Son of God on an equality with Mahomet and Confucius and discuss Christianity as "one of the religions" of the world, instead of men being compelled to see, as in the days of the early Church at Pentecost, the omnipotent power of God bearing witness to the name of His Son as the only Saviour for a lost world.

Again in mission work, the appeal to the senses and emotions of the soul accounts for the large percentage of converts who do not stand, and for the fleeting influence of much evangelistic work—as well as in many instances the excessive exhaustion of the worker, and oft-times his eventual "breakdown." A correspondent writes: "Is it not the exercise of the soulish, or natural man—the glow, feeling, emotion, and energy, in speaking to others publicly or privately—that causes *nerve exhaustion*? And is it not possible for the Spirit to quicken the truth without the strain, or wear and tear of the body? Or to tell out God's truth with no 'excitement,' and for God to breathe out His power in the words you speak, not through *you* so much as through your *testimony*, after it leaves your lips, and enters into the minds of others? It does seem as if more work could be done, and with far less fatigue, if my surmise be true."

A man may have naturally a "fiery" soul, and by that fiery soul sway and move the soul-emotions of others. But their faith then stands in the influence, or wisdom, of the man they have listened to, and not in the power of God. We can now see what Dr. Andrew Murray means when he says that the greatest danger which the Church or individual has to dread is the *"inordinate activity of the soul, with its power of mind and will."* The old Quakers used to call this "creaturely activity," and it is manifestly the energy of the creature being used in the service of God rather than the creature seeking in spirit to co-operate with the Holy Spirit given to him as the Gift of the Risen Son of God.

We find the intellectual man, with his

spirit yet unquickened, dealing with the eternal destinies of immortal souls. And we find the strong-willed man exercising his will, and dominant personality, over the consciences and lives of others! Schemes, therefore, to reach men and bring them to God by smoking concerts, musical attractions, lectures on popular subjects, etc., are but the outcome of various types of "soul" in men who desire to help others. Such men may be *regenerated,* but "governed by soul," and not knowing the Spirit of God dwelling in the spirit to energize them by His indwelling power and use them as messengers of God in the salvation of men.

But there is another section of the Christian Church—and a much smaller company—who, knowing the Spirit of God indwelling them, are "soulish" in a much lesser degree. These are they who have a mixture of "soul and spirit" in their religious experiences. They are not satisfied unless they *feel* the presence of God continually with them, in the realm of their self-consciousness. Consequently, although the Holy Spirit dwells in them, they often fall into the realm of the soulish life because they do not understand the spirit life and the actions of the human spirit in co-action with God.

The "soul" not only comprises the intellect and the emotions, but from the Scriptures it can be seen that the soul is the seat of the personality in its affections, power of joy or grief, etc. Thus it is written: "My *soul* is exceeding *sorrowful* . . ." (Matthew 26:38); "My *soul* doth magnify the Lord" (Luke 1:46); "Now is my *soul* troubled . . ." (John 12:27); "In *patience* possess ye your *souls*" (Luke 21:19); "*Vexed* his righteous *soul*" (2 Peter 2:8); "Beguiling *unstable souls*" (2 Peter 2:14). It is therefore clear that the idiosyncracies of the individual exist in the soul, as well as in the physical disposition of the body. And this shape of the soul, if we may use the expression, in its capacity for joy, love, grief, patience, etc., may be filled with a spiritual joy, from the Spirit-life of the Second Adam, poured out into the vessel of the soul; or filled with a soulish—or sensuous—joy, moving into the vessel of the soul from the lower life of the first Adam. In the latter case the believer, although indwelt by the Holy Spirit, is "soulish" to the degree to which the animal soul-life has play in the realm of these various capacities of the soul. He may cling to a soulish joy and live in the realm of his feelings or in the seat of his *self*-consciousness and not in the spirit, the place of the God-consciousness. If so, he will be among those believers who are always seeking for spiritual "experiences" in the *sense*-consciousness, instead of in the purity of the God-conscious realm alone—the regenerated human spirit.

At this point let us see how the spirits of evil work upon the soulish life in all its phases.

THE SOUL AND
THE POWERS OF DARKNESS

"If in your hearts you have bitter feelings of envy and rivalry, do not speak boastingly and falsely in defiance of the truth. That is not the wisdom which comes down from above: it belongs to earth, to the un-spiritual nature [Greek, psychical] *and to evil spirits"* (James 3:14–15, *Weymouth*).

In the *ASV*, as we have seen, the text runs, "This wisdom is not a wisdom that cometh down from above, but is earthly, sensual [*i.e.,* natural—the literal Greek is "pertaining to the soul"], *devilish* [margin of *ASV*: demoniacal]." This passage we have already referred to, but we quote it again as showing conclusively *the relationship of the forces of evil to the animal soul-life.* We have here no reference to the "works of the flesh" but to man's intellectual department— *i.e.,* the *soul,* and the words of the text show that evil spirits work upon the soulish part of the man *as certainly as they do upon his fleshly nature.*

It is startling to see the truth put so bluntly and to know that all bitter feelings of envy and rivalry in connection with the gaining or possession of *knowledge* are instigated by evil spirits, working upon the soulish life, and have their origin—as Fausset writes—in *hell*.

This is not very well understood by many true children of God. They may acknowledge satanic influence in the matter of gross sin and the manifestation of the "works of the flesh," but not in the realm of what they consider the highest part of the civilization of today. Back of this lies the unwillingness to recognize statements of the Word of God concerning the Fall and the utter sinking of the entire first creation into corruption and death so that even the "imagination" of the "thoughts of his heart"—*i.e., mental conceptions*—was seen by God to be "evil continually." And back of this total corruption again lies the poison of the Serpent, who obtained entrance through the avenue of the *desire for wisdom*.

In the progress of the renewal of the redeemed man, it is *to the interest of the forces of evil that any element of the fallen life, whether fleshly or soulish, should be kept active,* for as the believer becomes "spiritual" he more and more is united in actual spirit-union with the Lord of Glory. Hence more and more he escapes the power of evil spirits and becomes equipped to recognize them and war against them. But it must first be recognized clearly that the Fall was the result of believing the lie of Satan, the fallen archangel; and that when Satan succeeded, there entered the race of fallen man a poison which runs through every element of his being. This gives Satan power of access to every part of his tripartite nature, *i.e.* (a) the fallen spirit, dead to God, is open to the hellish dark world of spirits ruled over by the Prince of Darkness; (b) the soul, including the intellect, imagination, thought, will and affections, is governed by the life of the first Adam, which is fallen and corrupt; and (c) *body and soul* is therefore open in every department to the power of the Poisoner. Consequently, the Apostle John declares with blunt language that "the whole world lieth in the evil one" (1 John 5:19, *ASV*).

The fallen man not only has to be redeemed by the lifeblood of the Son of God, but he has to be *actually translated* out of the power of darkness into the Kingdom of God's Son—every department of his being, beginning with his spirit, ACTUALLY RENEWED stage by stage by deliverance from the power of sin and the animal soul-life. If the first creation was "fearfully and wonderfully made," then in truth the *re-creation* of the creature—utterly sunk into the animal soul and the animal flesh, and lifted again into the realm of spirit to have spirit-dominion over soul and body—is a wondrous work, which only the Triune God could accomplish. The Father gave the Son, the Son gave His life, and the Holy Spirit is giving Himself with patience and love to work out the will of the Trinity.

That the Prince of Darkness resists every step of the man's deliverance out of his thraldom is easy to understand, and it is necessary that we should know clearly the elements in the fallen creation which are open to his power. That he fully controls the unregenerate man is clearly shown in Ephesians 2:2–3, where the apostle says that the "children of wrath" doing "the desires of the flesh, and of the thoughts" (*i.e.,* soulish life), are wholly dominated by him. Then, when the spirit of the man has been quickened into life, and he has been delivered from the power of sin, the soulish life and elements in the physical body are still open to evil powers. For example—

(1) First in the soulish life, the soulish wisdom becomes "demoniacal" when evil spirits use it to accomplish their plans, *e.g.,* the enemy can arouse a mental prejudice, or preconceived idea—*unknown to the man*—and use it at a critical moment to *frustrate the work of the Spirit of God.* This working of the enemy through the mind of a believer, when the heart and spirit may be true to God, is a most serious fact in the

Church of God today, for through the various "ideas" of good men, the Spirit of God is sometimes hindered even more than through the unbelief and hatred of the world. Again, in the realm of the emotional soul-life, the adversary can so rouse the life of nature that the deep work of the Spirit of God is quenched or checked, and His voice unheard.

(2) In the physical body, the adversary can work upon the nervous system, and use the animal magnetism which is inherent in every human frame, as well as many other elements open to the powers of evil, in addition to "the works of the flesh" and what is generally called *sin*.

These elements are in the very make-up of the human vessel. On the part of the believer there should be a keen seeking of light from God on his complex being, that he may understand himself, and know how to act and walk in humble dependence upon the Risen Lord for protection from the evil one—a protection which can only operate as the man looks to the blood of Jesus, and in implicit obedience to the written Word keeps himself open to all truth which will give him light upon any possible ground he may have given to the spirits of evil to attack or gain admittance to mind or body.

For the powers of darkness are keenly clever in working alongside of or simulating "natural" conditions, either in temperament or disturbance of the bodily functions or frame,* and they watch for some physical or mental ailment to serve as the cover or as an "excuse" for their workings.†

---

*That is, the attack may be in the natural and physical realm, but not from it as the source.

†For full elucidation of this aspect of truth, see *War on the Saints,* a textbook on the work of deceiving spirits among the children of God.

CHAPTER 4

HOW "SOUL" AND "SPIRIT"
ARE DIVIDED

*"The word of God is living, and active,
and sharper than any two-edged sword,
and piercing even to the dividing of soul
and spirit, of both joints and marrow, and
quick to discern the thoughts and intents of
the heart . . ."* (Hebrews 4:12, ASV).

THIS remarkable passage in Hebrews
4:12 clearly sets forth the distinction
between soul and spirit, the need of the
"dividing" of one from the other, and the
means whereby this is done, so that the
believer may become a truly "spiritual"
man, living "according to God in the spirit"
(1 Peter 4:6). Pember points out, in regard
to this passage, that here the apostle
"claims for the Word of God the power of
separating, and, as it were, taking to pieces,
the whole being of man, spiritual, psychic

47

(soulish), and corporeal, even as the priest flayed and divided limb from limb the animal for the burnt offering. . . ."

Fausset writes, "The Word of God is 'living,' and 'powerful'—*energetically efficacious* (Greek)—'reaching through even to the *separation of the animal-soul from the spirit*, the higher part of man'"; "piercing even to the dividing of soul and spirit, of both joints and marrow, . . . distinguishing what is spiritual from what is carnal and animal in him: the spirit from the soul." "The Word of God divides the closely joined parts of man's immaterial being, soul and spirit. . . ." An image taken from the "literal dividing of joints, and penetrating to (so as to open out) the marrow by the priest's knife."

These words show how suggestive, and full of teaching, is the whole passage to the believer whose eyes are opened to the danger of the soul-life dominating him, instead of the Spirit of God acting freely from the shrine of his spirit.

The question at once arises in a believer who desires to be a spiritual man—"What am I to do? How can I discern what is soulish in my walk and service?" The text we are considering shows that we are to yield ourselves to our High Priest who has "passed into the heavens," and He, before whom "all things are naked, and laid open"

(Hebrews 4:13, *ASV*), will exercise His office of Priest and wield the sharp two-edged knife of His Word, piercing to the dividing of soul and spirit within us, discerning even the "thoughts and intents of the heart." "The Greek for 'thoughts' refers to the mind and feelings, and the word 'intents,' or rather 'mental conceptions,' refers to the intellect," again writes Fausset in his commentary.

The High Priest, who Himself became man, that He might be "a merciful and faithful high priest" (Hebrews 2:17), able to sympathize, and touched with the very feeling of our physical and moral weakness (Hebrews 4:15), is the only one who can take the sacrificial knife and patiently "divide" the soulish life from its penetration into thoughts and feelings, the intellect, and even mental conceptions. What a work to be done! How can the animal soul-life, penetrating the very "joints and marrow," be tracked and dislodged so that the spirit indwelt by the Holy Spirit may dominate, and every thought be brought into captivity to the obedience of Christ? Our High Priest will not fail nor be discouraged in bringing forth victory out of judgment in all those who commit themselves to His hands and trust Him to wield the knife of His living Word by the Spirit of God.

But what are the steps? What is man's part? How is the believer to co-operate with the High Priest in this great and delicate work?

(1) *By definite surrender* of the whole man as a burnt sacrifice laid upon the altar of the cross, with the entire consent of the will irrevocably given, that the High Priest, Christ Jesus, should by His Spirit bring the entire being into conformity to His death (Philippians 3:10), *i.e.,* that He should never stay His hand until the *animal-soulish life is "divided" from the "spirit,"* so that the man may become a vessel into which, and through which, the inflow and outflow of the Spirit of God may flow freely from the shrine of the spirit.

(2) *By continual, persistent, watchful prayer,* and searching the Scriptures, praying that the keen edge of the Word of God may be applied to all that is of the soulish life; the believer implicitly obeying the Word, right up to the light given, according to 1 Peter 1:22, *ASV,* "Ye have *purified your souls* in your obedience to the truth."

(3) *By the daily taking of the cross* in the circumstances of life, so that the believer has the entire victory over sin and the "works of the flesh," while the Spirit of God is doing the more minute work of separating the spirit from the soul and teaching the believer how to walk after the spirit.

How the separation between soul and spirit is carried out in those who thus lay

themselves upon the altar (the cross) and
trust the heavenly High Priest to use the
sword of His Word as a knife to do the work
in them, we see in the calls to the cross
given by the Lord Jesus to His disciples
when He walked the earth as man.

THE CROSS AND
THE SOUL AFFECTIONS

> *"He that doth not take his cross and fol-
> low after Me is not worthy of Me. He that
> findeth his life [psuche, soul-life] shall lose
> it; and he that loseth his life [psuche, soul-
> life] for My sake shall find it"* (Matthew
> 10:38–39, *ASV* and margin).

This passage occurs in the charge given
to the twelve when the Lord sent them forth
in His name. He warns them that "a man's
foes shall be those of his own household"
and shows that their first following Him in ✓
the path of the cross will mean a "sword" in
their family life, when the claims of Christ
and the family are not in accord. The
"sword" to divide the soulish and the spiritual in the affections generally comes in a
clash between the known will of God and
the will of the loved ones, which compels
the believer to "take his cross," *i.e.,* "go
forth even to crucifixion,* and follow the

---

*"We have become so accustomed to the expression 'taking up

Lord, even though it causes "variance" with
father or mother or the "own household."

It was so with Christ Himself. He who
had said, "Honor your father and your
mother" had to say, "Who is My mother
and My brethren?" when they judged Him
to be "beside himself" as He was occupied
with His Father's business. The taking of
the cross in this way, and the choosing to
be obedient to Christ before family claims,
means to the natural affections such suffering that it is as a sword piercing the
soul, so that in very truth the soul-life in
the affections is "lost," and the purified vessel of the "soul" in the aspect of its affections becomes open to the inflow of the love
of God by the Spirit, whereby the believer
loves the loved ones no longer for himself
but for God, and in and through God.

The lower life is exchanged for the higher,
i.e., the "soul" in its personality and vessel-
capacity remaining the same "soul," but
now dominated from the spirit by the Spirit
of Christ—the Last Adam—and not by the
fleshly soul-life of the first Adam (*cf.* 1 Corinthians 15:45–48).

In Luke's Gospel the sword-effect of the
cross in connection with the soul's affec-

one's cross' in the sense of being prepared for trials . . . that
we are apt to lose sight of its primary and proper sense here—a
preparedness to go forth even to crucifixion"—Fausset.

tions is more plainly defined, for the Lord uses the word "hate" and says, "If any man come unto Me, and HATETH not his father, and mother, and wife, and children, and brethren, and sisters, yea, and his *own life* also, he cannot be My disciple" (Luke 14:26). Here again the word "life" is *"psuche"—i.e.,* the animal or soul-life. Matthew gives us the test for the *will* in its choice of God or the loved ones as *first* in the words "loveth *more* than Me"; but Luke records the language used by the Lord which describes the ATTITUDE of the wholly devoted follower of Christ to *the soul-life in its permeating of the affections—an attitude which is necessary for their purification.* Such a believer must "hate" his "own life" (the *psuche*) *in its penetration to family relationships,* so that he may have *"soul"* divided from "spirit" in this sphere, and, in the "hating" and "losing" of his soul-life, find the higher and purer love-life of Christ which shall permeate the close family ties, ordained and honored by God Himself through His Son in human form.

THE CROSS AND SOULISH SELF-INTEREST

"If any man would come after Me, let him deny himself. . . . For whosoever would save his life [soul] shall lose it: and whoso-

*ever shall lose his life [soul] for My sake
shall find it"* (Matthew 16:24–25, *ASV*).

Later on Matthew again records a similar
statement by the Lord, but this time it is
drawn forth by Peter's words to Jesus in
regard to His cross. Peter had said, "Pity
thyself," but the Lord replies that the path
of following Him meant "DENY HIMSELF."
Here is the soul-life summed up in the
word *"himself,"* when shown in self-
centeredness in any form, *i.e.,* self-pity,
self-interest, self-shrinking from suffering;
in short, all that would make a man "save
his life" rather than go forward in divine
strength to pour out his "soul" unto death
for others.

The choosing of the path of the cross for
Christ's sake means the "losing" of the
fleshly soul-life, to have the pure divine life
of Christ in its capacity for sacrifice
"found" and poured out through the soul-
vessel for the blessing of the world.

The Evangelist Mark repeats the words
as given in Matthew's Gospel (Mark 8:34–
36). Luke does the same with the addition
of the word *"daily,"* showing that the cross
in connection with the outpouring and sacrifice of the soul-life needs to be of *daily*
choice and efficacy and is a distinctly different aspect of the cross to that given in
Romans 6 and the other Epistles, where

the death of the old creation is to be apprehended as a COMPLETED FACT, made true as the believer "reckons" himself "dead indeed unto sin" and "alive unto God in Christ Jesus."

THE CROSS AND SOULISH GRASPING OF EARTHLY THINGS

"Remember Lot's wife. Whosoever shall seek to gain his life [soul] shall lose it: but whosoever shall lose his life [soul] shall save it alive" (Luke 17:32–33, *ASV* margin).

Here we find again the same emphatic words repeated by the Lord, in connection with self-interest and the *natural* instinct of self-preservation and the self-grasping of earthly possessions. "Remember Lot's wife," says the Lord Jesus, as He points out the natural tendency of the soul-life—to turn back in the hour of danger to save one's goods and not to let them go.

The law of gaining the higher spirit-life is to "lose" so as to "gain." The soulish life seeks earthly treasures, but these must be renounced, and the "dividing of soul and spirit" in this connection will come about again by the attitude of the believer when in the vicissitudes of life the test comes. "They took joyfully the spoiling of their goods," is written of some in days of trial (Hebrews 10:34). This attitude to "possessions" is sometimes a greater manifestation of divine grace than the sacrifice of life.

The renouncing of the soul-life in its innate clinging to the things of earth is a necessity for the "gaining" of the Spirit-life of Christ, which, pouring into the vessel of the soul from the spirit (as the seat of the God-consciousness) brings with it such an assurance of abundance in God that earth's treasures are held lightly and are easily forsaken in the times of testing which come to all men.

The undue absorption of the children of God in "house" and "goods" to the neglect of the Kingdom of God is manifestly an aspect of the "soul" and not the spirit-life; and this clinging to or over occupation with the necessary affairs of earth needs the knife-work of the great High Priest in the "dividing of soul and spirit," so that the affections of His blood-bought ones may be set on things above, in fulfillment of the word: "for *ye died* and your life is hid with Christ in God" (Colossians 3:1–3, *ASV*).

THE CROSS AND
SOULISH SELF-LOVE

"He that loveth his life [soul] loseth it; and he that hateth his life [psuche—soul-life] in this world shall keep it unto life [zoe—the higher life] eternal" (John 12:25, *ASV*).

Here we have the contrast between the soul-life and the higher life of the spirit, manifested in and through the soul-personality, very clearly defined. The soul-life is now shown as summed up in SELF-LOVE: he that "*loveth* his soul"—which simply means *himself*. We have seen the soul-life penetrating family affections and manifested in self-pity, self-protection, the self-grasping of the goods of earth—in brief, summed up in "my family, myself, my goods"—with self-love in and through all.

All this, the Master says, means loss—eternal loss—for it all comes from the life derived from the first Adam, manifested through the personality of the soul, and prevents that "soul" from being dominated by the spirit and giving expression to the pure divine life of the Last Adam—the Lord from heaven.

Is it "sin" to keep it? Yes, WHEN THE LIGHT COMES, AND WE SEE THE TRUTH. *In a deeper sense also it is sin*—although unknown sin: for all the life of the first Adam—*i.e.,* the "natural man"—has been poisoned by sin; and even in those who apprehend "death to sin" as set forth in Romans 6, and in consequence cease to "walk after the flesh" in manifestation of the "works of the flesh," it penetrates into the realm of the affections, and shows itself in self-love, self-pity, self-grasping, and other phases of self-centeredness. This must be called SIN, although in a less discernible form, working through intellect, emotions and affections.

THE PATHWAY OF FREEDOM

"The love of Christ constraineth us; because we thus judge that one died for all, therefore all died; and he died for all, that they that live should no longer live unto themselves, but unto Him . . ." (2 Corinthians 5:14–15, *ASV*).

The work of dividing soul and spirit is done by the Lord Himself, through His Spirit wielding the Word of God as a living, active "sword" which penetrates to the inmost recesses of the immaterial being of man.

But THE MAN HIMSELF HAS HIS PART TO DO. The Spirit of God cannot carry out His work without the believer's consent and co-working. Briefly summarized, the conditions of cooperation on the man's side are as follows:

(1) *The believer needs to see* the necessity of the dividing of soul and spirit, and as the sacrifice is laid on the altar, definitely consent to the work being done.

(2) *The will of the believer* must be steadily placed on God's side in the experiential working out of the "dividing" as the circumstances of life require it.

(3) *The basis of the cross* as set forth in Romans 6:1–14 must be steadily main-

tained. As the believer reckons himself "dead indeed unto sin" (Romans 6:11), and actively carries out the command NOT to "let sin reign" in his mortal body, thus finding the "flesh" crucified with its "affections and lusts" (Galatians 5:24), so must he now reckon himself dead indeed unto sin in its more subtle forms through the soul-life, *i.e.*, the *evil* "self" conditions, such as inordinate self-love, self-pity, etc.

(4) The believer fulfilling these conditions must now carry out in practice his light, purpose, and faith, and steadily be faithful to all that he is shown by the Spirit of God, refusing deliberately all intrusion of the soul-life and choosing to open himself to the higher life of Christ in his spirit.

(5) The believer must seek in all things to "walk after the spirit"; to discern what is spirit and what is soul, so as to follow the one and refuse the other; to understand the laws of the spirit so as to walk in them and become in reality a "spiritual" man.

As the believer fulfills these conditions he becomes in truth a new man, for the power of the cross as the sword of the Spirit has been wielded by the hands of the heavenly High Priest, piercing to the dividing of soul and spirit; it has tracked the soul-life even to joints and marrow, to the inner recesses of the soul in the source of its activity and the very "marrow" of its affections; yes, it has even discerned the soulish life in mind and feelings and in the very conceptions of the mental powers. Now the believer more and more joyfully and easily walks according to the written Word and takes up the "cross" as brought to bear upon him *daily* in the providence of God. Apprehending with ever clearer vision the fact of his death with Christ upon the cross, the spirit of the man is more and more divided from the soul and joined in essential union with the Risen Lord who is a Life-giving Spirit—so that he becomes "one spirit" with Him and his human spirit a channel for the outflow of the Spirit of Christ to a needy world.

CHAPTER 5

THE SPIRITUAL CHRISTIAN

"He that is spiritual [pneumatikos] judgeth all things" (1 Corinthians 2:15).

"And the God of peace Himself sanctify you wholly; and may your spirit [pneuma] and soul [psuche] and body [soma] be preserved entire, without blame . . ." (1 Thessalonians 5:23, ASV).

IN this passage in Thessalonians we have, as it has already been observed, one of the only two which in English plainly declare the tripartite nature of man, also describing it in the due—and original—order. It is remarkable how frequently the order is changed by many children of God when quoting this verse in Thessalonians, as they pray that they may be "sanctified, *body,* soul and spirit," showing that the mind unconsciously describes the true conditions of the fallen creation—until the believer is illuminated by the Spirit of God and the spirit is brought back to its place of control, in thought as well as all the other activities of the man.

The apostle in his prayer for the Thessalonians gives comprehensively a picture of the "spiritual" believer, for he could pray no less for any of his converts than that they should be sanctified wholly; just as he wrote to the Colossians that he labored that he might present every man "perfect" or "full-grown" in Christ—the word he used denoting "grown to the ripeness of maturity."* "I pray God," he says, "your whole spirit and soul and body be preserved blameless" (*KJV*). The being "preserved blameless" or "entire" follows the being "sanctified wholly." And this briefly means:

(1) *As regards the spirit:* The Triune God, who is Spirit, taking up His abode in the shrine of the spirit of the man, who is first quickened in spirit by the Holy Spirit through the redemptive work of the Son.

(2) *As regards the soul:* The Triune God dwelling in the spirit manifesting Himself through the vessel of the soul—or personality—of the man, in (a) a will wholly one with the will of God, (b) an intellect renewed and illuminated by the Holy Spirit,

---

*Colossians 1:28–29. See Conybeare's note.

and (c) emotions under the complete control and usage of the man, guided by that same Spirit.

(3) *As regards the body:* The Triune God abiding in the spirit, manifesting Himself through the avenues of the soul, keeping the body under complete mastery (1 Corinthians 9:27), with every member yielding quick obedience as a "weapon of righteousness" (Romans 6:13, *ASV*), thus making the outer man—the body—verily a sanctuary of the Holy Ghost (1 Corinthians 6:19).

This is the "spiritual" believer, grown to the "ripeness of maturity"; sanctified wholly in spirit, soul and body, and needing to be "preserved entire" and blameless—not *faultless*—by the God of Peace dwelling in the central shrine of his being.

HOW THE SOULISH MAN BECOMES SPIRITUAL

But how, we may ask, does the believer pass from the "soulish" stage to become actually a "spiritual" man? "The 'spiritual' is the man distinguished above his fellowmen as he *in whom the spirit rules,*" writes Fausset. The "ruling of the spirit" does not only mean the Spirit of God ruling the carnal, or the soulish man, but the regenerate spirit made stronger than soul and body, so that it rules over both as it is indwelt and strengthened by the Spirit of God, ac-

cording to the prayer of Paul for the
Ephesians, that they might be "strengthened with might by His Spirit in the inner
man"—*i.e.,* in the *regenerate human spirit*
(Bishop Moule).

The "spiritual man" is he who "walks after the spirit" and "minds" the spirit—the
spirit being thus so co-working with the
Holy Spirit that the Life-giving Spirit of the
Second Adam is able freely and fully to
animate the faculties of the soul—*i.e.,*
mind, imagination, reason, judgment—
quicken the members of the body (Romans
8:11) and manifest through them His fullest and highest will.

For this to come about, the believer must
not only apprehend the *negative* side of
God's dealing as depicted in Hebrews
4:12—the dividing of "soul" from "spirit"—
but the *positive* side depicted in 1 Thessalonians 5:23, showing the God of Peace
"sanctifying" the whole, by taking possession of and working through the spirit and
seeing that the soul and body fulfill their
proper functions.

"He that is joined unto the Lord is *one
spirit*" (1 Corinthians 6:17), wrote the
apostle. "Ye also were made dead to the law
through the body of Christ; that ye should
be *joined to another,* even to Him who was
raised from the dead" (Romans 7:4, *ASV*).
Here is set forth clearly the "joining" or

union with Christ in the spirit, which is the purpose and outcome of the work of the cross. This union with the Risen and Ascended Lord can be only in *spirit,* and IS EXPERIENTIALLY REALIZED as the SPIRIT OF THE BELIEVER IS SEPARATED FROM THE ENWRAPPING OF THE SOUL; for, as Stockmayer observes, the Risen Lord cannot be said to be the Bridegroom of the *soul;* the soul—the personality of the man—can only be the vessel through which the Lord manifests His own life, bringing forth, in union with the believer's spirit, "fruit unto God."

The "spiritual" man, therefore, is one in whom, through the dividing of soul and spirit by the Word of God, THE SPIRIT HAS BEEN FREED from the entanglement of the soul, or, as Bromley (who wrote in 1774) says, raised out of its "embrace," and joined to the Lord in union of essence—spirit with spirit—*one* spirit—so that the soul and body may serve as vehicles for the expression of the will and life and love of the Lord Himself through the believer.

In the light of this, the contrast between the "works" of the "flesh" and the "*fruit*" of the "Spirit," described in Galatians 5:18–24, is very striking. The "flesh" *works,* and works out to the surface its repulsive manifestations; while in the man who knows both the Romans 6 aspect of Calvary—the crucifixion of the flesh—and the dividing of soul from spirit by the Word of God, the spirit united to the Lord *brings forth FRUIT*— spontaneous manifestations of life in the form of fruit: fruit manifested in and through the soul (personality) in its various forms of love, joy, peace, long-suffering, kindness, goodness, faithfulness, meekness and self-control.

The word "self-control" being mentioned as one of the fruits of the Spirit shows that the Spirit of God uses the "self"— personality or "soul"—of the man as His means of control. The personality, as meaning self— *the soul*—is therefore not to be destroyed or suppressed, but is ennobled as it becomes a vehicle for expressing the Spirit of Christ dwelling within. In brief, the "fruit of the Spirit," in "love, joy, peace," means *love manifested through the "soul," but derived from the Holy Spirit in the human spirit* instead of from the soul-life.

There are many passages in the Scriptures describing the various "soul"-faculties in activity and deriving their animation from the spirit. We read of the being "*fervent* in spirit" (Romans 12:11); the *purposing* in the spirit (Acts 19:21); the spirit of *faith* (2 Corinthians 4:13); *love* in the spirit (Colossians 1:8); all these spirit-activities being manifested through the avenue of the soul—*the personality*—of the man: the "wisdom" through his mind; the "purposing" through his will; the "love" through his affectional part; the "joy" through his emotional senses, but *springing* from the eternal depth of his *spirit* and not merely from his senses alone.

THE LAWS OF THE SPIRIT LIFE

It is at this stage that it is vitally important that the believer should know the laws of the spirit and how to walk after the spirit, lest he fail to co-operate with the Holy Spirit and give opportunity to the deceiving spirits of Satan to ensnare him with counterfeits of the true spirit-life, produced in the soul-realm, which he fails to recognize as spurious; for their object is to draw him to walk unknowingly in the soul-sphere again. The spiritual man—with his spirit liberated or "divided" from the soul—is one who walks by or is governed by the *spirit*, not by his soul or body. But this does not mean that he cannot be entangled in the soul-life again, if through ignorance of the laws of the spirit he fails to let the spirit rule. He must know how to discern specifically what is from the *spirit*, the *soul* or the *body* in his experience; how to keep the spirit free and open to the Spirit of God; and what *condition* of spirit is necessary for continuous co-operation with the Holy Spirit. He needs to be able to recognize and deal with the attacks of evil spirit-beings upon his spirit to hinder fellowship with God or to press it down into the soul, paralyzing its action and causing passivity of spirit. Failing this, they will seek to drive his spirit beyond a sober activity—the entire object being to prevent or hinder continuous resistance to their attacks.

For walking after the spirit (1) the believer must know what is spirit, and how to give heed to the demands of the spirit and not to quench it. A weight comes upon his spirit, but he goes on with his work, putting up with the pressure; he finds the work hard, but he has no time to investigate the cause, until at last the weight becomes unendurable and he is forced to stop and see what is the matter—whereas he should have given heed to the claims of the spirit at the first and in a brief prayer taken the "weight" to God, refusing all pressure from the foe.

(2) He should be able to read his spirit and know at once when it is out of co-operation with the Holy Spirit, quickly refusing all attacks which are drawing his spirit out of the poise of fellowship with God.

(3) He should know when his spirit is touched by the poison of the spirits of evil: by the injection, for instance, of sadness, soreness, complaint, grumbling, faultfinding, touchiness, bitterness, feeling hurt, jealousy, etc.—all direct from the enemy to

the *spirit.* He should resist all sadness, gloom and grumbling injected into his spirit, for the victory life of a freed spirit means joyfulness (Galatians 5:22). This touching of the spirit by the various things just named is not a manifestation of the "works of the flesh" when the believer is one who knows the life after the spirit; *however, they will quickly reach the sphere of the flesh if not recognized and not dealt with in sharp refusal and resistance.*

(4) He should know when his spirit is in the right position of dominance over soul and body, and so is not driven beyond due measure by the exigencies of conflict or environment. There are three conditions of the spirit which the believer should be able to discern and deal with:

(a) The spirit depressed, crushed or "down."

(b) The spirit in its right position, in poise and calm control.

(c) The spirit drawn out beyond "poise" when it is in strain or driven.

When the man walks after the spirit, and discerns any one of these conditions, he knows how to "lift" his spirit when it is depressed; and how to check the over-action by a quiet act of his volition, when it is drawn out of poise by over-eagerness or the drive of spiritual foes.

The human spirit may be likened to the

electric light. If it is in contact with the
Spirit of God, it is full of light; apart from
Him it is darkness. Indwelt by Him, "the
spirit of man is the candle of the Lord"
(Proverbs 20:27). The spirit may also be
likened to elastic: when it is bound, or
pressed, or weighted, it ceases to act, or to
be the source of power and "spring," so to
speak. If a man feels weighted, he should
find out what the weight is. If he is asked,
"Is it your body?" he would probably say
"No," but that he "feels bound inside." Then
what is it that is "bound" or "weighted"? *Is
it not the spirit?* The spirit can be com-
pressed or expanded, bound or free. The
possibilities and potentialities of the human spirit are only known when the spirit
is joined to Christ, and "by reason of use"
is made strong by the Holy Spirit to "stand
against the powers of darkness."*

THE SPIRITUAL MAN IS "FULL-GROWN" IN CHRIST

The "spiritual" man is also described by
the apostle as "full-grown" in Christ, and in
the first letter to the Corinthians we have a
striking contrast drawn between the spiritual and carnal believer. The carnal—or
fleshly—believer can only be fed with

---

*For fuller light on this aspect of the walk after the spirit, see
War on the Saints, from which this portion is extracted.

"milk," the simplest element of the gospel, whereas to the "full-grown" or "spiritual" man can be given the "deep things of God," things which cannot even be spoken "in words which man's wisdom teacheth, but which the Spirit teacheth, interpreting spiritual *things* [not truths, be it noted, but things—facts—substances—as real as things material on earth] to spiritual men" (1 Corinthians 2:10, 13, *ASV* margin).

The apostle makes it clear also that the "soulish"—or "man of soul"—cannot receive these "things" of the Spirit any more than can the fleshly "babes in Christ" (1 Corinthians 2:14–3:1), for to the soulish intellect and wisdom they appear nought but foolishness. None but those who are spiritual can discern them and *examine* (*ASV* margin) them—for they can be "examined" as truly as material things! The "spiritual" man "examines all things," for he is able by the Holy Spirit to penetrate to *the inner spiritual source of all things* and pierce through the veil of sense and sight to the spiritual verities lying at the back of all things; but the "soulish" man—*i.e.,* the man who can use only his *natural* intellect, who cannot pierce further than the intellect can go—he can examine all things in the natural sphere and no more!

"The spiritual man is ripe in understanding," writes the apostle. And if we carefully

examine all the references in Paul's epistles to the "spiritual" man, and the "grown" man, we shall see how the dividing of soul and spirit in the believer is the condition of reaching the stage called "spiritual" or of "full growth." The "full-grown" stage is again and again connected with the knowledge, teaching and discernment of spiritual things, all having to do with the soul.

"We speak wisdom among them that are full grown" (1 Corinthians 2:6, *ASV*); "Be not children *in mind* . . . but *in mind be of full age*" (1 Corinthians 14:20, *ASV* margin); "Teaching every man in all wisdom, that we may present every man perfect [same Greek word as rendered "full grown"] in Christ" (Colossians 1:28); "Solid food is for full-grown men, even those who by reason of use have their senses exercised to discern . . ." (Hebrews 5:14, *ASV*). "Let us, therefore, as many as be perfect [or "ripe in understanding," "perfect" being the antithesis of "babe" and the same Greek word as "full grown" in 1 Corinthians 2:6], be thus minded" (Philippians 3:15), writes the apostle in his letters. For the Colossians, he prays that they may be "filled with the knowledge of His will in all spiritual wisdom and understanding" (Colossians 1:9); and it is the "spiritual" man who is bidden to restore a brother overtaken in any trespass, for he only can exercise the heavenly wisdom required for faithfulness in dealing with sin from the standpoint of God, while loving tenderly the erring brother (Galatians 6:1).

Again, to the Ephesians the apostle writes, "Till we all attain unto the unity of the faith, and of the knowledge of the Son of God, unto a *full-grown man,* unto the measure of the stature of the fullness of Christ" (Ephesians 4:13, *ASV*). Here again is knowledge linked with full growth and the fullness of Christ! The "unity of the faith" which should characterize the mystical Body of Christ, and bring about its "full stature," cannot be manifested until each of the individual members reaches the full-growth stage and becomes a "spiritual" man; and again, each member cannot thus become "spiritual" until he apprehends the separation of soul and spirit, so that the spirit may be fully joined to the Risen Lord and the "soul-vessel" in its intellectual and other departments be energized and dominated by the spirit from the sphere of the God-consciousness, not from the lower life of the first Adam.

THE SPIRITUAL MAN IS "MADE PERFECT IN LOVE"

The word "perfect"—or "complete"— which is "full-grown" in 1 Corinthians 2:6, *ASV,* and joined so often with the mind or knowledge by Paul, is joined with *love* by

the Apostle John. He speaks of the believer
being "made perfect in love" (1 John 4:18),
and tells how "perfect love casteth out fear,"
and "love made perfect" gives "boldness in
the day of judgment." The First Epistle of
John shows the "spiritual" man, therefore,
as one with the *affections* of the soul fully
possessed with the love of God, and so
entirely as to be completely filled full with
love flowing from Him who dwells in the
spirit. "God dwelleth in us and His love is
perfected in us," writes the apostle; *i.e.*, the
vessel of the soul is *perfectly filled* with
divine love, so that up to its measure and
capacity it is "complete" with the love of
God, and so filled that "fear" has no place
and no room.

But John's language means even more
than the fact that the divine love of Him
who dwells in the spirit of the believer can
flow freely through the soul-vessel. He is
really describing the life in the Spirit of the
spiritual man, *i.e.*, what living and dwelling
in the sphere of "God-consciousness"
means. "God is love," he writes, "and he
that *abideth in love* abideth *in God,* and
God abideth in him" (1 John 4:16, *ASV*).
The "spiritual" man who lives and walks in
the spirit of love is thus "abiding in God." If
"fear" or "hate" comes in, he has *descended
to the soul-realm* and admitted some element of the natural soul-life, or else,

through the attack of evil spirits, he has ceased to co-work with God in his spirit. Upon discerning it he must at once go to the cross, to submit the soulish element to its severing power—while Godward he calls it "*sin*" and seeks the application of the cleansing blood according to 1 John 1:7, at the same time resisting the powers of darkness and taking up once more the "whole armor of God" for victory.

THE SPIRITUAL MAN IS "PERFECTED INTO ONE" WITH ALL BELIEVERS

The "spiritual man" is perfected into one spirit with others in Christ. The word "perfect" used in 1 Corinthians 2:6 was also used by the Lord Jesus in His high priestly prayer to describe the union between His redeemed ones—which lay as the burden on His heart on the eve of His going to the cross to make that union possible. "As Thou, Father, art in Me, and I in Thee, that they also may be *in Us* . . . that they may be one, even as We are one; I in them, and Thou in Me, that they may be *perfected into one* . . ." (John 17:21–23, ASV). The essential union which exists between Father and Son—the union of essence in spirit with spirit—is the union of the believer each with the other who is IN God. The language of the Lord is unmistakable. He said, "That they may be one, *even as WE are ONE!*" This means Father and Son, dwelling in the *spirit of the believer,* by the Holy Ghost, in perfect—or complete—union. Of necessity it also means the *same union of spirit* with other believers. The "spiritual" man is therefore not only one with Christ in God, who is Love, but he finds the same union with the same God abiding in others. Therefore, he cannot be fully abiding in God if he in any degree admits the soulish life of nature which is manifested in (1) divisions, (2) partiality (James 3:17), or (3) factions (Galatians 5:20, *ASV*).

THE SPIRITUAL MAN
"WALKS IN THE LIGHT"

Again, it is of the "spiritual" man that the Apostle John writes, "If we walk in the light, as He is in the light, we have fellowship one with another, and the blood of Jesus Christ, His Son, cleanseth us from all sin . . ." (1 John 1:7). The walking in light can only be by the man living in the sphere of God-consciousness, where God dwells in his spirit. Any descent into the realm of the soul may be likened to having that spirit which is joined to the One who *is* light sinking into an opaque vessel—which brings a cloud or film over it and obscures the light. The believer abiding in God who *is* light abides and "walks" in light, and in that light finds "fellowship" with God and with others who dwell in light. Meanwhile, the blood of Jesus goes on cleansing continuously from all unknown sin which may unconsciously touch the abiding one by any intrusion of the "soul-life," or from contact with sin in the world around.*

"God is light, and in Him is no darkness at all." "He that *loveth . . . abideth in the light.*" This is the Ascension life, or life hidden with Christ in God, of which the Apostle Paul writes. It was spoken of to the disciples by the Lord Jesus in His farewell words in the upper room at Jerusalem, and was brought into their real experience by the Holy Ghost on the Day of Pentecost when the Spirit of the glorified Jesus entered their spirit. They were then lifted up out of the soul-realm into spiritual oneness with the glorified Lord. Abiding in Him and He in them—this caused the "world" to take note. And a multitude believed! They saw the oneness of the Spirit-filled company "made perfect in love," with all "fear" cast out; they saw them walking in such light that sinful selfishness, like that manifested by Ananias, could not be allowed to exist among them!

In light of all this, and what it means to Christ and His Church—that all the mem-

---

*For all known sin in the matter of trespass, 1 John 1:9 is the remedy.

bers of His Body should thus become "spiritual" and adjusted (or perfected) into their
place in union with the Risen Head—the
importance of the believer understanding
the difference between "soul" and "spirit"
cannot be overestimated. For upon his
ceasing to live "after the flesh"—*in the
sense-consciousness*—depends his growth
into a fully "spiritual" man, *i.e.*, a man able
to understand his spirit and to discern and
examine spiritual things. A man indwelt by
the Triune God and sanctified wholly, by
the complete liberation of his spirit from
the domination of either soul or body—and
walking whereunto he has attained—is yet
pressing on to fuller "perfection" or com-
pleteness (Philippians 3:15–16).

How long should be the stage between
the first step of the new birth and becoming full-grown in the life of Christ—in the
sense of the spirit being liberated through
its union with the Risen and Ascended Lord
and having complete domination of soul
and body—we cannot clearly say. The language used by the apostle to the Corinthians, and again by the writer to the Hebrews, suggests blame that many believers
had continued too long in the stage of ba-
byhood, "yet carnal," and needing milk on
account of their weak spiritual life, when
they should have been teachers, leading
other "babes" on into full growth. The baby-

stage can evidently be protracted or short-
ened and need not be measured by ordinary periods of time. Probably the length is
determined by the measure of truth apprehended, and the knowledge and self-sur-
render of the believer. At all events, the
language of the writer to the Hebrews
makes it clear that the attitude of the believer has much to do with his progress.
Writing to those he had just rebuked by
saying that they had become "dull of hear-
ing" and needed to be taught again the first
principles of the gospel, he says: "Where-
fore leaving the doctrine of the first principles of Christ, let us *press on unto full
growth* . . ." (Hebrews 6:1, *ASV* margin)—
almost the very words of Paul to the
Philippians in chapter 3, where he tells of
his own eager pressing on, not assuming
that he was "already made perfect," although he would also say "Let us who
are . . . perfect"—*i.e.,* complete, or full-
grown—be thus minded in pressing on to-
wards the goal of the upward calling of God
in Christ Jesus.

THE SPIRITUAL MAN AND
THE "SPIRITUAL BODY"

The "spiritual body," referred to in 1 Corinthians 15:44, with which the believer will
be clothed in the resurrection, is a logical
outcome of the spiritual stage we have been

considering. "That is not first which is spiritual," writes the apostle, "but that which is natural; then that which is spiritual" (v. 46, *ASV*). The babe in Christ is "yet carnal," but by his understanding of Romans 6 he soon ceases to walk after the flesh and walks after the Spirit. Then he understands the "dividing of soul and spirit" and becomes a "spiritual man" with mind renewed, his soul and body a vehicle for God to express Himself through him. Now the original order of the tripartite man is restored, in the sense of:

1. The Holy Spirit ruling in the liberated spirit (*the seat of the God-consciousness*),

    with

2. The soul—or personality—as the vessel (*the seat of the self-consciousness*),

    and

3. The body as the slave (*the seat of the sense-consciousness*).

Now the man is truly "spiritual"—or, to put it more crudely, we might say he is a "spirit" dwelling in the vessel of the "soul," and this likewise is encased in a physical, mortal body. The language of Paul clearly shows that the full redemption of the body awaits the appearing of the Lord from heaven. "We ourselves groan," he writes, "waiting for our adoption, to wit, the re-

demption of our body" (Romans 8:23, *ASV*);
"We wait for a Saviour, the Lord Jesus
Christ: who shall fashion anew the body of
our humiliation, that it may be conformed
to the body of His glory" (Philippians 3:20–
21, *ASV*); "We would be clothed upon, that
what is mortal may be swallowed up of life"
(2 Corinthians 5:4, *ASV*). The body is, therefore, still a "natural" body, a mortal body, a
vessel of clay (2 Corinthians 4:7). And not
until sown in the earth at death—or changed
in the twinkling of an eye at the Lord's
coming—is it raised "a spiritual body."

But the "spiritual" man who lives under
the rule of the Holy Spirit day by day may
have an increasing "earnest" of the coming
redemption of the body. For as he walks in
the spirit, his body shares in the life-giving
power of the Spirit, according to Romans
8:11, where the apostle declares, "If the
Spirit of Him that raised up Jesus from the
dead dwelleth in you, He that raised up
Christ Jesus from the dead *shall give life
also to your mortal bodies* because of His
Spirit that dwelleth in you" (*ASV* margin).
The power of the reality of this "quickening
of the mortal body" by the very same Spirit
of the Father which "raised up Jesus from
the dead" can be known only as far as the
soul-life of nature is *continuously* "lost" by
the power of the cross (Matthew 16:24–26),
for the mortal body can only be quickened

by the Holy Spirit when the Life-giving Spirit is free to energize soul and body.

The apostle's suggestive words in 2 Corinthians 4:10–12, *ASV,* have to do with this stage of the believer's life. Just as the soul-life has to be "lost" to find the Spirit-life inflowing from the Holy Spirit, using the soul-capacity and faculties, so the same principle of "loss" for "gain" must work in the mortal body. Therefore, it is written: "Always bearing about in the body the dying of Jesus, that the life also of Jesus may be manifested in our body."

The loss of the carnal-life animating the soul was gradual, giving place to the inflow of the Spirit-life as the believer yielded to the dividing of soul and spirit, brought about by the wielding of the sword of the Spirit by the heavenly High Priest. Likewise, the "dying of Jesus" works continuously in the mortal body as the believer follows on in the way of the cross, "pressed, perplexed, pursued, smitten down"—yea, "pressed above measure, despairing even of life" (2 Corinthians 1:8–9), so as to cast him upon the God who raiseth the dead, that he may prove the "life of Jesus" manifested in the sustaining and quickening of the mortal body. This "losing" of life, to "gain" the life of Jesus, is brought about by the Holy Spirit as the believer follows on to know the Lord. "We who *live,*" writes the apostle, "are always *delivered* to death . . . that the life also of Jesus may be manifested in our mortal flesh. So then *death worketh in us, but life in you*" (2 Corinthians 4:11–12, *ASV*).

Painful as it is to the "mortal flesh," the "spiritual" man, able to "examine" these deep things of God, can see that the inworking of death and life means two results of vital importance to the Lord and His people: (1) That when the life of Jesus can freely flow from the sanctuary of the spirit *through the soul-faculties,* quickening the "mortal body" with unhindered power, it means *life to others,* as well as to the believer himself—a quickening life to the whole Church of Christ, as depicted by the Lord in His promise of rivers of living water. (2) That this quickening of the mortal body is the "earnest of the Spirit," whereby *the body itself is being prepared* for the hour when "what is mortal may be swallowed up of life," even as the apostle writes, ". . . He that *wrought us* for this very thing is God, who gave unto us the earnest of the Spirit" (2 Corinthians 5:4–5, *ASV*).

SOME DANGERS FOR
THE SPIRITUAL MAN

The believer who has become really "spiritual"—that is, with his spirit ruling soul and body—does not at that time pass out of the realm of conflict but enters upon a more subtle phase of it, as set forth in Ephesians 6:10–18. The man who is said, in Ephesians 2:6, to be "seated with Christ in the heavenlies" is afterwards described as "wrestling" with spiritual hosts of wickedness in "high places," particularly in the form of the "wiles" of the devil.

This indicates that the spiritual believer in conflict *has mainly to watch against subtle spiritual wiles of spirit-foes,* who are seeking to entangle him in matters connected with the spiritual realm, rather than in the conflict between flesh and spirit described in Galatians 5:17.

In this phase of conflict, the wiles of the powers of darkness are mainly directed toward getting the spiritual man to walk, in some degree, *after the soul* and not after the spirit; that is, to be influenced by and to walk by anything in the *realm of the senses,* instead of in the spirit in co-operation with the Holy Spirit of God.

It is essential, then, that the *spiritual* believer should understand that deceiving spirits of Satan can create a counterfeit of the human spirit in the realm of the soul. They do this by getting access to the outer man by guile and then producing emotions in the man other than those of the spirit. When these other emotions—which possibly *appear* spiritual—get a hold, they may become strong enough to silence or over-power the true spirit-action. If the believer is ignorant of the tactics of the enemy in this way, the true spirit-action is easily allowed to sink into disuse by the man following the counterfeit spiritual feelings, thinking he is "walking after the spirit."

When the true spirit-action ceases, the evil spirits may suggest that "God now guides through the *renewed mind*." Such is an attempt to hide their counterfeit work-ings and the man's disuse of his spirit. At the same time comes counterfeit light to the mind, followed by counterfeit reason-ing, judging, etc., and the man thinks he has light from God because he is unaware that he has ceased to "walk after the spirit" and is now walking after the natural *mind*.

Another danger for the spiritual man lies in the subtle attempts of the deceiving spir-its of Satan to get him to walk after the flesh (*i.e.*, body), in the belief that he is still walking in the spirit, by creating feelings in the *body* which the man thinks are "spiri-tual." To defeat these wiles, the believer should understand that all *physical* con-sciousness of supernatural things, even undue physical consciousness of *natural* things, should be refused. Both divert the mind from "walking after the spirit" and set it upon the bodily sensations. Undue physi-cal consciousness is also an obstacle to the continuous concentration of the mind. In a spiritual believer an "attack" of "physical consciousness" made use of by the enemy may break concentration of the mind and bring *a cloud upon the spirit*. Therefore the body should be kept calm and under full control. For this reason, excessive laughter and all "rushing" which rouses the physical life to the extent of dominating mind and spirit should be avoided. Believers who desire to be "spiritual," and of "full age" in the life of God, must avoid excess, extravagance and extremes in all things (*cf.* 1 Corinthians 9:25–27).

Because of the domination of the physical part of the man and the misunderstanding of supernatural experiences felt in the body, *the body is made to do the work of the spirit* and is forced into prominence which suppresses the true spirit-life. Under such conditions the *body feels* the pressure, *feels* the conflict, and becomes the "sense" in the place of the mind and spirit. Believers should learn to discriminate and know how to discern the true feelings of the spirit, which are neither emotional (soulish) nor physical. (See, for example, Mark 8:12; John 13:21; Acts 18:5, *KJV*.)

Through ignorance, a large majority of believers walk "after the soul," *i.e.*, their mind and emotions, under the impression that they are "walking after the spirit." Because of what this means—depriving the believer of vital spirit power—the satanic forces use all their wiles to draw him to live in his soul or body, sometimes flashing visions to the mind, making presentations to the mind during prayer or giving exquisite sensations of joy, buoyancy of life, etc., to the body.

To depend upon supernatural things given from outside, or experiences in the sense realm, checks the inward spiritual life. By the bait of "experiences" in the senses the believer is drawn to live in the outer field of his body instead of living in the true sphere of the spirit. Then, ceasing to act from his center, he is caught by the outer workings of the supernatural in his circumference and loses—quite unconsciously—his inner *co-operation* with God. Then his spirit, which is the organ of the Holy Spirit in conflict against a spiritual foe, drops into abeyance and is ignored, because the believer is occupied with the sense-experience. Consequently, it is practically out of action, either for guidance or for power in service and conflict.

There is a serious danger arising out of the human spirit acting apart from co-operation with the Holy Spirit. When the spirit has been "divided" from the soul and become dominant, it is then open to become influenced by deceiving spirits in quite another way. Supposing in one of the ways already indicated, or otherwise, the man has ceased (unconsciously) to co-operate with the Holy Spirit, and is still guided by his spirit, he is liable to think his own masterful spirit is an evidence of the power of God, because in other directions he sees the Holy Spirit using him in winning souls. Under that delusion, he may have a flood of indignation inserted into his spirit, and he pours it out, thinking it is all of God. But others, with real discernment, are conscious of a harsh note which is clearly not of God. Such an experience may easily take place in conflict, as well as in speaking, if the praying one is not watchful—the energizing power being demoniacal and either influencing the spirit directly or by way of the soulish emotions.

This influence on the human spirit by evil spirits counterfeiting the divine workings in the man himself—because he is out of co-working with the Holy Spirit—needs to be understood and detected by the believer who seeks to walk with God. He needs to know that *because* he is spiritual his spirit is open to two forces of the spirit realm. If he thinks that only the Holy Spirit can influence him in the spiritual sphere, he is sure to be misled. If it were so, he would become infallible. But he needs to watch and pray, and seek to have the eyes

THE SPIRITUAL CHRISTIAN   89

of his understanding enlightened to distinguish the true workings of God from the
counterfeit.

The believer who is "spiritual" must pon-
der deeply the unveiling of the heavenly
warfare given in Ephesians 6 and strive to
know in its fullest extent the experiential
meaning of the "whole armor of God" which
he is to "take" and use in the "evil day" of
specific onslaughts by the foe.

The burden of the Spirit of God at this
present time is the perfecting, or *full ripen-
ing into maturity,* of the members of the
Body of Christ, so that His appearing may
quickly take place and the millennial reign
of Christ and His co-heirs be ushered in.
For the peace of the world and the discom-
fiture of Satan—who will then be cast down
into the pit, and the kingdoms of the world
become the Kingdom of our Lord and of His
Christ—for that, "Lord Jesus, come quickly.
Amen."

> Made free! Made free in Jesus:
>   Deep planted in His death,
> He liberates His Life power,
>   And breathes His Spirit's breath,
> Then, waxing strong in spirit,
>   With force of quickening life,
> The soul and body governed,
>   Its members cease from strife.

Made free! Made free in Jesus:
    Joined to the Risen One,
By conflict prayer you triumph,
    And claim His victory won.
Freed with His glorious freedom,
    Above the darkness rife;
For now the law of sin and death
    Is conquered by His life.

                    M.M.

APPENDIX*

"SOUL-FORCE" VERSUS "SPIRIT-FORCE"

1

SOME LIGHT UPON THE PERILS OF THE LAST DAYS

"THE forces of *psuche* [soul] are arrayed against the forces of *pneuma* [spirit]" —this is the expressive sentence used by a correspondent in India to describe the conflict in the unseen realm in these solemn days. This is his description of the real issues in *India* at the present time, but to those able to distinguish between "soul" and "spirit," the words just as vividly depict what is taking place in Great Britain as well as in the East. The situation is undoubtedly challenging. The Church of

---

*The following papers first appeared in *The Overcomer*, in 1921 through 1923.

Christ in her advance in the things of God is meeting with new phases of testings, and all she has hitherto known seems inadequate to meet her need. Fresh light from God the Holy Spirit is therefore an imperative necessity, and this He is giving as new situations arise.

"The forces of *psuche* are arrayed against the forces of *pneuma*"! What does this "soul-force" mean? Our correspondent writes at length as follows:

"The forces of the pit have gone forth to deceive the whole world (Revelation 12:7–12). The consequence is that great upheavals are taking place in the political world. It is important for us to take account of these happenings, as they vitally affect the Church of Christ.

"I once met a man in North India who had access to the highest circles of society in Simla, the summer seat of the government of India, who told me one evening of his connection with the mahatmas in India and in other countries of Asia. He said that he knew of great political events weeks and months before they came to pass. 'I do not depend for news on telegrams and newspapers. They only record past events; we know events before they take place,' he said. How can a man in India know of the events happening in London and vice versa?

"It was explained to me that it was

through 'soul-force' being projected by men who knew the secret of the mahatmas. *What is soul-force?* To the *believer* taught by the Spirit of God, in the light of the Word of God it is seen to be the *power of the pit* projected upon the nations of the world to deceive them, so as to bring about catastrophic changes.

" 'Soul-force' is a word whose charm and magic is only known in the East. It is the power believed to have been exercised by holy men, known as mahatmas, who were the spiritual leaders in India in centuries gone by and who are credited with supernatural powers as much today as in ages past. It is said to have the capacity not only to energize but to control the will of the people.

"To illustrate the potency of this word in the Indian mind, it is sufficient to point to the revision of the Treaty of Sevres, under which all that was lost to Turkey has to be restored. A greater triumph of one Eastern nation over all Western nations combined cannot be imagined. The explanation given, and *believed in by millions in India,* is expressed in the word 'soul-force.'

"This 'soul-force' is believed to be cultivated by prayer, fasting and religious meditation. The Muslims point with pride to their gatherings for prayer in their mosques. Consider the mass of Muslims at prayer in the great Jumna Mosque of Delhi, where a hundred thousand followers of Mohammed assemble inside the mosque, with a still larger crowd engaged in prayer outside. It is *here* that 'soul-force' is generated! *In the mosques of India,* which number thousands upon thousands, devout Muslims meet three times for prayer every day. It is *here* that the hidden springs of Islam lie. Every Muslim believes that the secret of world-power is in prayer, and what he believes, he practices. They 'pray,' and so (they believe) the council of European nations is set aside. What a lesson to Christendom!

"And how is soul-force cultivated among the vast *Hindu* population of India? If the gatherings of Muslims for prayer are large, those of Hindus, when they meet for devotional exercise at their great festivals, are ten times larger. The Hindus point with pride to their sacred places of pilgrimage, where they assemble by hundreds of thousands. At the great Magh Festival at Allahabad, millions of Hindus assemble every seven years.

"*Prayer*—an exercise of devotion which unites Hindu and Muslim into *one common action: to generate 'soul-force' in order that it may be projected upon Western nations to undermine their power and prestige in the East.* It is the greatest revolt known in history! . . ."

*   *   *   *

There is a passage in Pember's *Earth's Earliest Ages* which throws light upon this matter. He writes that the man who would generate "soul-force" must "so bring his body under the control of his own soul *that he can project his soul and spirit* and, while living on this earth, act as if he were a disembodied spirit." The "man who attains to this power is called an 'adept' and . . . can consciously see the minds of others. He can act by his 'soul-force' on external spirits. . . . He can subdue ferocious, wild beasts and send his soul to a distance," and he can "exhibit to his distant friends his spiritual body in the likeness of that of the flesh." We read that "the development of these faculties . . . can only be compassed by a long . . . training, the object of which is to break down the body to a complete subjection and to produce apathy in regard to all the pleasures, pains and emotions of this life. . . ."

The whole tenor of Indian religious life undoubtedly develops these soul-powers, for what can be the effect of intense "prayer" fixed on a given object by a hundred thousand men who know not the gospel of Christ but the "projecting" of soul-forces, directed by the god of this world, upon the object desired.

"Soul-force" versus *"spirit-force."* What does this mean in *England?* Just this: that

the same development of *psychic* power is
taking place all around us, both knowingly
and *unknowingly,* bringing into action
forces which are at the disposal of the invisible powers of evil. "The forces of *psuche*
are arrayed against the forces of *pneuma.*"
√ What are the "forces of *psuche*" but the
"natural man" drawing out of his nature
latent powers which are not of the Spirit of
God. And the "forces of *pneuma,*" what are
they? The power of God Himself as "Spirit"
brought into action through the spiritual
man, born of the Spirit, walking after the
Spirit and praying to God on the ground of
the blood of Calvary. (See Revelation 8:3–5
as an example.)

How this unwitting bringing into action
of psychic force can affect spiritual believers has come to me in a recent letter. The
writer says: "I have just come through a
terrible onslaught of the enemy. My whole
body was in a state of collapse from hemorrhage, heart palpitation, panting and exhaustion. It suddenly burst upon me while
at prayer to pray against all psychic power
exercised upon me by [psychic] 'prayer.' By
faith in the power of the blood of Christ, I
cut myself off from it. The result was remarkable. Instantly my breathing became
normal, the hemorrhage stopped, exhaustion vanished, all pain fled and life came
back into my body. I have been refreshed

and invigorated ever since. God let me know in confirmation of this deliverance that *my condition was the effect of a group of deceived souls* who are in opposition to me and are 'praying' about me! God has used me in the deliverance of two of them, but the rest are in an awful pit. . . ."

This is not the only instance which has come to my knowledge within the last few months of the fresh dangers coming upon spiritual believers—through the deepening tribulation conditions which are coming to pass throughout the whole inhabited earth. Through these other instances it appears that this generation of soul-force under the guise of Christian prayer is most likely to take place in those who have had great supernatural experiences but have in some way opened themselves to evil spirits. These Christian souls seem, in some way, to get what might be called a *fanatical spirit of insistence* that other believers should come into the same experience that they have had. And if these others in any way refuse to seek these experiences, or appear to these souls to be a block in the path of others obtaining these supernatural manifestations, they direct, as they think, "prayer" upon them, that they should be punished by God with judgment or that they should be *compelled* to yield to what these souls call "the truth."

But this is very much like the disciples who said to the Lord, when they came to a village where they would not receive Him, "Lord, wilt Thou that we command fire to come down from heaven and consume them?" And the Lord replied, "Ye know not what manner of *spirit* ye are of." God never uses compulsion to force any soul into receiving Him, even for their own benefit. God the Holy Spirit recognizes the human responsibility of a man's own choice as to whether God shall save him or not.

So we would earnestly warn God's servants—truly *God's* servants—who seem to be concerned about others who will not seek their own particular line of "blessing." And we entreat them rather to commit these other believers to God and not to lay themselves open to the danger of generating soul-force by directing what might be called *evil prayers* upon them. In any case, it behooves all who give themselves to *intense* prayer to carefully avoid *praying for others what they think is the "will of God" for them.* And above all things, never to *direct* "prayer" *upon* others but always upward *toward* God, thus leaving those for whom they pray free from the possible danger of soul-force working upon them through the aerial currents of the hour.

As an example of this a minister writes: "We have recently had a convention in this

town. One of the speakers was out to en-
force his own supernatural experience on
others—his own particular line of 'blessing.' I was the subject of much 'prayer' on
this line, and I have since seriously felt the
effect. . . . This concentrating of the mind
(*i.e.*, soul-force) in prayer on something that
one *wants* is fraught with evil. . . ."

Let us remember that true Spirit-born
prayer has its origin in the *spirit* and that *it
is not the mind concentrating upon something the person desires under the cover of
"prayer" language.*

2

THE WORLD ISSUES OF TODAY

SEVERAL letters have reached me concerning the brief paper "Soul-force Versus Spirit-force" given in our last issue. A
ministerial reader describes it as being ep-
ochal in importance, while others confirm
from personal experience some of the statements made, showing how truly the present
increase of Satanic activity is hastening the
world on into the tribulation period foretold
in the Word of God.

But I am asked to give more light on the
meaning of "soul-force" and why in its

present development it is fraught with such peril to the children of God. To explain clearly what "soul-force" consists of and why it is now being aroused and used by the powers of darkness in the last great phase of the warfare against the truth of God, we need first to go to the Scriptures. Under the illumination of the Spirit of God we will see what is taught therein on the subject of "Soul and Spirit."

Dr. Andrew Murray's explanation of what the "soul" or *psuche* is, and its relation to the spirit and the body, is very clear. Man consists of (1) spirit, (2) *soul,* and (3) body— "The *spirit* is the seat of our God-consciousness; the *soul,* of our self-consciousness; the *body,* of our world-consciousness. In the spirit [of the believer], *God* dwells; in the soul, *self;* in the body, *sense. . . .*"

The distinction between the *soul* and the *spirit* is of the greatest moment, for it is because of our not knowing this that the devil is able to deceive and mislead even children of God.

There are passages in the Scripture where it appears that "soul" and "spirit" are synonymous. But an understanding of Christian experience—that when one reaches the full stature of Christ, the "spirit" penetrates the "soul" so that they become practically one—makes this synonymous use of the words clear.

"God is a *Spirit*." They who "worship Him must worship Him in *spirit . . . ,*" said Christ. Every human being has a spirit, albeit a spirit separated from God through the Fall. It is the "spirit" which has to be rekindled by the light of God and regenerated by the impartation of the life of Christ. Thus the man is "recreated" or "born" *from above* (John 3:3, margin). There is no spark of the Divine in man by nature since the Fall but *a spirit which is fallen and needing regeneration or a new birth.*

This is the crux of the whole matter and of far more than academic importance. A mistake here is eternal in its consequences. The Fall and the need of regeneration through the substitutionary death of Christ cannot be a question of "opinion" upon which men may differ. Right *here* is the bedrock division of the human race into those who are born of God and those who are not. Right *here* is the one point of the devil's concern and the fundamental issue of every kind of "ism" under the sun.

The "soul" is the seat of our "self-consciousness," writes Dr. Murray. It comprehends all our "moral and intellectual faculties," also "consciousness . . . self-determination, or mind and will." "What occurred in Adam's fall," he writes, was that "the 'soul' (*i.e.,* the self) had to decide whether it would yield itself to the spirit, by it to be linked with God and *His* will, or to the body and the solicitations of the visible." In the Fall the soul *"refused the rule of the spirit and became the slave of the body. . . ."* Thus, "because the soul is under the power of the flesh, man is spoken of as having *'become flesh' . . ."* and *"all the attributes of the soul,"* therefore, belong to the flesh and are "under its power."

This makes the matter quite clear. In the natural man, the development and use of "soul-force" means *the development and use of all the "attributes of the soul" while in its fallen condition* and therefore apart from God, even though it might appear to be in the service of God. Truly regenerated believers must face the fact that since "soul-power" or "soul-force" has its source in the soul, or self—and not in the spirit, which in the Christian is the place of the Divine indwelling—the Spirit of God *does not use the natural forces* of the soul for the carrying out of the purposes of God, though He does use the faculties of the soul in a consecrated man as a vehicle for expression of the life of God.

How important this fact is we find Dr. Murray emphasizing in the following solemn words: "The greatest danger the religion of the Church, or the individual, has to dread is the inordinate activity of the soul, WITH ITS POWER OF MIND OR WILL. For many, the 'soul' has been so long accustomed to rule that even when . . . it has surrendered to Christ, the soul imagines it is now its work to carry out that surrender." So "subtle and mighty is this spirit of self" (or soul) that "the flesh, . . . even when the soul learns to serve God, still asserts its power, *refuses to let the Spirit alone lead* and, in its efforts to be religious, is still the great enemy that ever hinders and quenches the Spirit. . . . What has been begun in the Spirit . . . very speedily passes over into confidence in the flesh."

Here we see the meaning of the words used by our India correspondent to depict the *world-issues* of the close of the age. It is the old battle described by Paul in Galatians 5:17: "The flesh lusteth against the Spirit, and the Spirit against the flesh," and the "carnal *mind* is enmity against God" (Romans 8:7, *cf.* Colossians 1:21). "Flesh" and "Spirit" are in radical opposition and always will be, even when the "flesh" is manifested in the form of "soul," *i.e.,* through the natural powers of mind and will, etc., inherent in the natural man. These are referred to in the list of "works of the flesh" under the words "idolatry, *witchcraft* [magical arts, *Conybeare*], hatred, variance, wrath, strife, *seditions, heresies*" (Galatians 5:19–21)—all activities of the soul-powers under the power of the flesh.

But now let us look at the matter from the standpoint of world-issues rather than in individual experience. Why can it be said that the world-conflict is becoming a question of "forces of *psuche*" (or soul) versus the "forces of *pneuma*" (or spirit)? To get light on the causes underlying this, we must again go back to the Eden tragedy and see what the fall of Adam meant and note the Serpent's objective, which is nearing its climax at the present hour. For we have not clearly understood how deep and tragic were the results of the Fall, nor what Adam carried with him into his fallen condition, nor realized that the God-given powers which Adam possessed in his sinless state then became open to use by the Tempter.

The gilded bait held out to Eve in the temptation was "Ye shall be *as God*" (Genesis 3:5). This was God's very purpose for the sinless pair before they fell. It seems that the word "likeness" in Genesis 1:26 signifies "to *become* like," indicating that the wonderful potentialities breathed into Adam, constituting the image of God, were meant to be developed in a process which would "end in man being like his Creator"* in dominion and rule over all things. How tragic, then, that God, who alone could

---

*E. McHardie.

rightly develop and guide the use of these powers, should be shut outside the wonderful being He had created. It is more terrible still that the very potentialities inherent in mankind should now lie open to the hand of His enemy.

We cannot now trace through the centuries all that has followed in this particular aspect of the Fall. We see references in the Scriptures again and again which indicate that the Archenemy of God and man knew how to use the resources he had gained and how "sorcerers" and "magicians" with abnormal powers were to be found linked with the powers of evil. It was reserved for the "time of the end," in which we live, for Satan's objective in Eden to be brought to its full manifestation. His purpose is to obtain the rule of the whole inhabited earth, and we are told that for a brief period he will be allowed to obtain his desire through a super-man he will endow with abnormal powers. Therefore the words are strikingly true of the present hour that "THE FORCES OF PSUCHE ARE MASSING AGAINST THE FORCES OF THE SPIRIT." For it is through *the fallen soul-powers* of men that the whole world will be prepared and made ready to accept the rule of the Antichrist. It means that for a time *God will be ruled out of the universe.* The potentialities given to sinless man in Eden, which when developed would have made him "like God" in power of rule and dominion, will become active to such a degree that man in his fallen condition will believe he is "like God" and exercise these powers under the control and instigation of the devil. Spiritists already boldly say that "Man possesses all the attributes hitherto ascribed to Deity . . . ," and Dr. Gratton Guinness wrote years ago that the apostasy would "take the perverted form of the fallen life of Adam, assuming what belongs only to partakers of the divine nature."

This throws light upon the present time in a remarkable way. How rapid has been the spread of the apostacy from the faith of the gospel among the leaders of the professing Christian Church—the result of the use of the fallen "soul-powers" under the unsuspected instigation of the enemy. In other directions the great theme is "Psychology," with "discoveries" of psychic forces undreamt of by mortal man, so filling the minds of men that they are indeed like "children blown round by every shifting current of teaching," led "cunningly toward the snares of misleading error" (Ephesians 4:14, *Conybeare*), little thinking that they are helping to fulfill a great worldwide scheme of the devil.

The story of the great plot of Satan the Master Strategist to capture men of science, men of business and men of religion must be left to another paper. Suffice it to say here that the scheme was to lead men to "discoveries" of "natural phenomena" under the name of "Psychic Science." A list of some of these "discoveries" is given by a writer on prophecy,* to which many more recent ones could be added. How they counterfeit in the soul-realm the wondrous life of God in the spirit cannot but strike those who know anything of the latter, and it is in this present development and increase of the use of the powers of the soul that peril lies for the children of God who are really "spiritual" but ignorant of these latent powers in the human frame.

3

THE PSYCHIC DISCOVERIES
IN THE LAST DAYS

"THE greatest danger the individual has to dread is the inordinate activity of the soul with its powers of mind and will," said Dr. Murray. This danger is intensified a thousandfold at the present time, through the advance made by those who term themselves "researchers" in Psychic Science,

---

*E. McHardie in the "Apostasy" pamphlets.

having led multitudes into knowledge of the hitherto undreamt-of forces latent in the human frame. The danger to the Christian desirous of walking after the spirit and being a channel for the outflow of the Spirit of God is very real, for even when a man becomes regenerate and has the life of God in his spirit, *through ignorance he may be using "soul-force," even in his mission work for God.* This may account for the transient results in some missions, more than we know.

But now let us endeavor to get a bird's-eye view of the dangers which we are attempting to point out under the term "soul-force." There is no writer who appears to have given such full information on the dispensational aspect of the subject as the late Mrs. McHardie. However, her valuable books are out of print, unavailable for the very hour for which they were written.*

---

*Some years ago the late Dr. Rudisill, having read these books, determined to see the writer. He accordingly took the long journey to Aberdeen for the express purpose of doing so and found the devoted authoress living alone in one room at the top of a house, doing her own work, because she had spent all her financial resources in publishing her message. Dr. Rudisill said that he found her a veritable encyclopedia of Biblical knowledge, a skilled scholar in the Hebrew and Greek languages. Later, she had a stroke and died in a nursing home, apparently leaving no one able to carry on her work. The plates of some of these books were offered to me after her death, but I was unable then to take advantage of the offer. The facts I set forth in this paper are gleaned from Mrs. McHardie's writings—J.P.L.

It is remarkable that in these closing days of the age, the book of Genesis should be so much contested by the devil, in his endeavor to overthrow its authority. The reason undoubtedly is that it not only contains the basic truth of the Fall and of the gospel of redemption, but *it also holds the key to all the problems of the present time.* It is so in the present instance. As we have pointed out already, the gilded bait offered to Eve in the temptation in Eden was "Ye shall be as God"—which was the very purpose in the heart of God in His creation of man. The point we need to grasp is this: (1) That the very attributes of the soul, now being brought to light by "psychical research," were placed in the sinless Adam for the express purpose of their development in fellowship with and for the purposes of God; (2) That the Tempter knew of these potentialities in the sinless Adam and desired them brought into action under his control instead of God's—hence the temptation to Eve; (3) That when Adam fell into awful separation in spirit from God, *all these latent powers fell with him* and became open to the control of the Tempter.

In a previous paper, we referred to the great plot of Satan, the Master Strategist, to capture (1) men of science, (2) men of business and (3) men of religion. This was made known by a medium under the direction of the evil spirits controlling her. Up to that time, said the controlling spirit, they had only succeeded in reaching the "noncritical part of humanity," and scientists, with some exceptions, stood aloof. We see the results at the present time in the numbers of scientists caught in the great deception, through the specious plea of "investigation" into a "natural science."

From this history of Spiritism we learn that the first stage of advance into conditions which enabled the spirits to break through into communication with man* was the discovery of Anton Mesmer, somewhere about 1778, from which has come a knowledge of what is called today *"Mesmerism."* Following Mesmer, we read that numbers of his converts made continuing "discoveries," producing phenomena which almost seemed incredible. But it was when Mesmer assumed the position of a man of science, appealed to the scientific world to examine "natural phenomena," and declared that he wanted for his "discovery" the "unqualified approval of the most scientific men" of the age, that the satanic scheme of capturing the men of science succeeded. For psychical researchers admit that Mesmerism is *"the rock from which*

---

*That is, apart from the long and difficult training of the "adept" referred to on page 95.

all mental sciences (including Christian Science) were hewn."

A list of some of the "discoveries" which followed the obtaining by Mesmer of the basic knowledge of the mysterious forces latent in the human frame shows how amazingly the movement advanced once men had obtained the key. In 1784, a pupil of Mesmer discovered "clairvoyance" as the result of mesmeric sleep and incidentally stumbled upon "Thought Reading." Then ancient books were studied for further knowledge, and it was seen that these "secrets of nature" had already been made known to a few. But now through Mesmer and his pupils the time had come for the advance of the movement—which in the end would re-engulf the world in darkness. Hypnotism, Neurology and Psychometry—the discovery that the mind can act outside the human body and that the "psychometric sensitive" can read the past like an open book—and numberless other "discoveries" followed as the years went by. Then came a discovery called "Statuvolism," signifying a peculiar condition produced by the *will,* in which the subject can "throw his mind" to any distant place, and see, hear, feel, smell and taste what is going on there. Then, through a revivalist preacher somewhere about 1847, came a discovery which he called "Pathetism," which caused him to leave the ministry to devote himself to the investigation of the "trance." Large numbers became magnetically affected at his lectures, the discoverer attributing these trances to *the power of "self-induction inherent in human life."* By this the mind could withdraw itself from the consciousness of pain and cure diseases.

At first, scientific men only followed up these "discoveries" as *branches of Natural Science,* and no attempt was made to connect spirit agency with the phenomena, all *teaching and doctrine being carefully withheld by the spirits.*

Then came the development of the plot to capture "men of business," which is assuming such wide dimensions today. The plan was to show how to put these "discoveries" to practical account for success in business and other pursuits. To this end, through wide advertisement, books were offered showing how to develop "The Power Within." Businessmen everywhere were urged to use "mind power," or mental magnetism, to attract friendship and success and to develop a "strong, magnetic, attractive personality."*

---

*This part of the plot is going forward by leaps and bounds even at the present time. A correspondent has just sent me copies of some papers which he says are flooding the mail in America, advertising books under the titles of *Personal Power, or Your Master-self; Creative Power, or Your Constructive Forces; Faith Power, or Your Inspirational Forces; Regenerative Power, or Vital Rejuvenation*; etc., etc.

Then followed the further carrying out of the plot, in the endeavor to reach "men of religion." How successful this has been is to be seen in the veritable landslide of professing Christian teachers absorbing the demon teachings of rationalistic views of the Bible, especially the objection to the atoning work of Christ, which is the main burden of all doctrines of demons.

This subtle undermining work by the deceptive spirits of Satan is now reaching its climax, and we can see how section after section of the leaders of the people have been captured by the enemy. The strategy has been masterly. "Men of science" led the way, and now "men of religion" have *capitulated to science* (falsely so-called), led astray by the Deceiver of the whole inhabited world.

We are undoubtedly reaching the high tide of the foretold "falling away" from the Faith. The momentum is increasing rapidly. The hand of the Archenemy of God and man is on the helm. The world is rushing to the dark hour, when, for a brief period, Satan will actually be the "god of this age," ruling through a super-man whose "parousia" cannot long be delayed.

Today "discovery" is following discovery until it is difficult to keep pace with the announcements in the daily press. "*Psychoanalysis,*" for example, is now a recognized "science," bluntly described, however, by a Canon at the Church Congress, as a "dabbling in dirt to an unnecessary degree!" And "teachers" galore are coming forth, each one with some fresh "teaching" from this whirlwind of psychic madness, leading the unwary away from the true gospel of Christ.

The purpose of the present psychic flood is plainly discernible by those who have some knowledge of what *"the days of Noah"* meant to his generation, so that a Flood to destroy all flesh was a necessity for the preservation of the race—through the one family that was clear of the prevailing corruption. It will be found ultimately that all phases of psychic science are *a definite substitution for some aspect of the gospel of Christ,* even to the point of UNION WITH INVISIBLE BEINGS as a counterfeit for the Christian's union with Christ. As the tide rushes on, it will be seen eventually that the latter is the main objective of all the purposes of Satan, so as to bring about the same corruption "as in the days of Noah."

The children of God must now know, for their own safety, *the difference between "soul" and "spirit."* They must know the possibility of ignorantly using *"psychoanalysis"* in dealing with the personal problems of others, instead of leading such souls to the cross for deliverance, in reliance upon THE INDWELLING POWER OF THE

HOLY SPIRIT. Yes, and in "warfare" against the devil himself there can be an *actual development of soul-force,* unless there is a deep work of the cross continually applied to the old Adam life, with a real life-union with the Risen Lord by the Holy Ghost.

"Soul-force" versus "Spirit-force" is the battleground today. The Body of Christ is, by the energy of the Holy Spirit within her, advancing heavenward. The atmosphere of the world is thickening with psychic currents, behind which are massed the aerial foes. The only safety for the child of God is an experiential knowledge of the life in union with Christ wherein he or she dwells with Christ in God, *above* the poisonous air in which the Prince of the power of the air carries on his work. The blood of Christ for cleansing; the cross of Christ for identification in death; the power of the Risen, Ascended Lord by the Holy Ghost, continually declared, laid hold of and wielded—these alone will bring the members of the Body through in victory to join the Ascended Head.

4

"THE SON CAN DO NOTHING
OF HIMSELF"*

THE meaning of "soul-force" can be
briefly defined as that which has its
origin in the soul and "spirit-force" as that
which has its origin in the spirit. The soul
is the medium for the outworking of both.
Soul-force is manifested through the faculties of the soul, and spirit-force is *manifested through the faculties of the soul likewise.* Let me try to explain it crudely thus.
Draw three sections, one above the other.
Mark the top one "spirit," the center one
"soul," and the lowest one "body." Then
draw an arrow passing down from the spirit
into the soul and then outward. This suggests the Holy Spirit in the human spirit
passing down and out through the faculties of the soul. Or draw an arrow going up
from the body section into the soul and out
through the faculties of the soul. In the
first you have spirit-force coming from God
energizing the soul; in the second you have
soul-force or power arising from the flesh
into the soul and out. The soul, as the

---

*A conference address. It is specially given here as describing,
in more simple language, the distinction between "soul" and
"spirit" referred to in previous articles.

central compartment, is the medium for both spirit-force and soul-force, and we can only tell which force is in action *by its fruits.* (See Matthew 7:16–17.)

I have said that soul-force, *as soul-force,* has its origin in the soul. More correctly, it rises from the body or animal life—this the Bible calls "flesh." There are great discoveries at the present time of powers in the soul such as our fathers never dreamed of. These forces have their origin in "flesh" and not "spirit," even though they do not appear so, for the soul is under the power of the flesh until the regenerated spirit rules by the power of the Holy Spirit dwelling within. He desires to control and use the soul faculties. For instance, either the *mind*—one of the faculties of the soul—is energized and animated by soul-force, or it is renewed by the Holy Spirit and energized by Him through the human spirit. The danger today is *the counterfeit in the soul realm of everything in the spiritual realm.* Through ignorance there has been a developing and using of these psychic forces, thinking them to be spiritual. But the word spoken by Christ is the test. He said, "It is the Spirit that quickeneth." *Only that which comes from the Holy Spirit through your spirit has its origin in God.* The latent powers of the soul are not divine—though some think they are. For example, some say that the "gift of healing" is in the *soul,* requiring development by those who have it. A clergyman writes, "This power is sometimes spoken of as 'animal magnetism,' sometimes as 'psychic power.' . . . This power *when dedicated to God* becomes a 'gift of the Spirit.' . . ." But surely the true gifts of the Spirit must come from God, who is Spirit, *via the spirit* and not the soul.

Again, in connection with the seeking of "manifestations" as an evidence of a believer having received the "baptism of the Spirit," methods have been used to bring these about *that synchronize with the methods of mesmerism,* and thus counterfeits have broken into the true Church of Christ. In other cases, believers have had a true influx of the Holy Spirit into their human spirit, and then through ignorance they have developed the psychic power latent in the human frame and brought about a mixture in their own life and service for God. For example, if a chorus is sung over and over again, they can bring a meeting into a psychic condition in which those present become incapable of intelligent thinking or of any decisive action of the will.

Thus, on a floodtide of psychic force in the world today the demons are carrying out their plans and purposes. "*It is the Spirit that quickeneth,* the flesh profiteth nothing." Every child of God is governed in all service—preaching, teaching, working—either by the Holy Spirit or by the psychic force of which we speak. It is the *spirit* that is regenerated—"a new spirit will I give you." Fausset says that the spirit is the shrine where the Holy Ghost dwells, and it is the organ through which He works. When He comes in and renews the spirit and dwells there, He then renews the mind and gains control over the faculties. As we walk in the Spirit and fulfill the conditions of His working, we become "spiritual" in all our actions. Everything touched will have a spiritual stamp; every faculty will be changed, quickened, uplifted. The believer becomes a "new man" and not only a new man but one who has the life of God in his spirit. Through the renewal of the mind, in due season, confused thinking passes away, and the mind becomes clear.

"The flesh profiteth nothing." How true it is in spiritual work. If it is animated by the flesh-life of the soul, there is no *fruit.* Toil as you may—no fruit! The reason is that it is "soul," energized by the life of nature, and therefore it "profits nothing." Vast toil and little fruitage! It is quite a fair exegesis of these words to say that if the "flesh" profits nothing, soul-force also profits nothing.

Let us look at some passages in John's Gospel and note the Lord's words about His own attitude as to reliance upon Himself and His own "powers"—which in His case were sinless powers. Our Lord had spoken about "eating His flesh" and "drinking His blood" (John 6:53–58), and His disciples said it was a "hard saying." It was in connection with the apprehension of spiritual truth that the Lord said that the "flesh" profited nothing. This is a very "hard saying" to the flesh and to the natural man who is unable to receive the things of the Spirit.

How marvelous it is to read that the Lord Jesus Christ said *"the Son can do nothing of Himself."* In no case did He originate His own activities. He did, He said, just what He saw the Father do— *"the Father dwelling in Me doeth His works."* There should be, in our measure, a continuous waiting upon Him for every step taken, until we can see what is from Him and what originates in ourselves. Then we may know the co-working of God in all our words and work.

The Lord Jesus said again, "As I hear, I judge." "I receive not honor from men." "I came not to do Mine own will." "I seek not Mine own glory." That was the position He took, and it is the position we are to take— entire dependence upon God. Again the Lord said, "No man can come to Me except the Father draw him" (John 6:44).

The danger today, for the true children of God, is the development of psychic powers in ignorance of their existence. There is also peril through the widespread teaching on psychology. Children are now to be saved from their "weaknesses" by psychic means, not by conviction of sin, conversion and regeneration. Even children of God need to be careful lest they take a psychological view of themselves, and while trusting God on the one hand, become so occupied with the "laws" of spirit, soul and body as to practically forget reliance upon the Holy Spirit Himself, whose office it is to take of the things of Christ and reveal them unto us. In the great supernatural movements of today there is a vast amount of psychic power. I have just received a letter from abroad concerning a great healing movement. The writer says, "It is all a dead failure. There are thousands upon thousands who have come, but it is failure, and what can you expect if the leader who 'lays hands' on others smokes and drinks whiskey!"

Let me close with a few points as to how soul-force can be a danger in the Christian life. There can be soul-force in relation to the *will*. The Lord liberates the will and energizes it, but it must be energized by the Spirit and not by the flesh. There is a possibility of soul-force in *will-prayer*. There can be a bringing of human will power to bear upon another person, through soul-force energizing the will. In ignorance of this danger, some believers project their thoughts onto the person they are praying for, saying that such and such a one "shall" do this or that. To avoid the possibility of soul-force prayers, we should be careful always to pray upward in a prayer directed to God. Every prayer should be directed Godward and should never be a telling the Lord what to do for somebody else. We may pray that God will direct them in what to do, but we ought not to say that they "must" do what *we think* is God's will they should do or even that they "shall not" do what we know is wrong. We are members of one Body. But we are each of us responsible to God only, and before Him we must stand or fall.

Then there is the danger of the drawing out of psychic forces in *worship*. The Lord said, "God is a *Spirit*, and they that worship Him must worship Him in spirit and in truth." What means then all the cultivation of the sensuous in the churches? Why do some people, living a worldly life all the week, become so happy because they have gone to church on Sunday? Is it not that through the music and other influences they have been made happy and comforted? They have been soothed, but the question is, *have they been truly convicted of sin and regenerated?* Is it wrong to have music? Not at all. There is a worship of God in song. But think of the psychic elements in the worship of the Roman Catholic churches! Dr. Andrew Murray points out that the ordinary activities of the soul easily intrude into worship. He adds that people little think that one reason why they do not get victory over some sin is *because they yield to the soul-life in the religious part of them.* They yield to self (flesh) in their *worship* and thus keep alive and active some fleshly sin, fed from a quarter they little suspect. They think they have done away with the "flesh" and cannot understand why these things remain. *The strength of the "sin" lies in the activity of the soul in its worship of God.* It is "flesh" under cover of the religious life. What must be dealt with first is our approach to God. He must be worshiped in spirit and in truth, *"for the Father seeketh such to worship Him."*

The present danger of the *spiritual* believer is the danger of soul-force. There are currents of thought sweeping in all directions. Many are caught in them and are not on guard against such currents. You can cut yourself off from them absolutely by taking your place in the death of Christ, asking that it shall come between you and all the atmospheric forces that are abroad at this time.

Let us ask ourselves whether our minds have been really renewed. Are they illuminated and energized by the Spirit of God, or

have we only the mind of the natural man?
The rationalism of today is not going to be
dealt with by intellectual arguments but *by
spiritual power and by prayer.* Let us pray
that the Lord will teach us how to live and
walk after the Spirit. With a renewed mind
may we learn to discern the difference between soul and spirit. "For the Word of God
is quick and powerful . . . dividing between
soul and spirit," so that the soul-life is
dealt with at the cross, and we become
"spiritual."

5

CALLING THE PSYCHICAL "SPIRITUAL"

IT is said of the "Beast" in Revelation 13:5
that, inspired by the Dragon, he would
be allowed to speak "blasphemies," and "he
opened his mouth in *blasphemy* against
God, to *blaspheme* His name and His tabernacle . . ." (v. 6). So rapidly are all the
characteristics foreshown as accompany-
ing the manifestation of the Antichrist coming to pass at the present hour that it is
difficult to keep pace with the need of unveiling them for the protection of those
whose names are written in "the Book of
Life of the Lamb slain from the foundation
of the world" (v. 8).

Especially are the *blasphemies* against God becoming more manifest in the appropriation of some of the most sacred elements of the gospel of Christ for the conveyance of demon-doctrines and demon-power. The climax of blasphemy is surely when the Lord's Table, instituted to show forth *His death* till He come, is made to be the table of demons by attributing to it magnetic and "psychic" power. This, by a bishop, in a book just published,* is said to be the "science of the sacraments" which is obvious to those who have "developed *psychic faculty.*" Supposedly, a "priest" is "an almoner to distribute His [the Lord's] *'force'* to the people." These "forces" are "being transmuted or materialized *within his very body*" as they "accumulate inside the surplice." There is also "a constant and vigorous *emission of power* from the magnetized stones upon the altar and from the crosses and candlesticks." And "particularly when incense is used, there is always a large attendance of the holy angels, and the *wondrous forces perpetually flowing from them* are caught and utilized for the congregation when suitable vestments are worn to act as *conductors. . . .*"

This "divine force," says the writer of the book teaching this "science of the sacra-

---

*In 1922 by the Theosophical Publishing House.

ments," is "a definite scientific fact." It is "often spoken of as the grace of God" and is "just as definite as steam or electricity." It is indeed "much more powerful in that it works upon the *soul*, the *mind*, the *emotions*. . . ."

On every side, the word "psychic" and "psychical" is to be met with in connection with religious teaching, often from leaders in the professing Christian Church. For instance, the *Archbishop of Caledonia* [Scotland] writes in an English paper: "A great discovery is being made in the *psychic* world."

"Our *psychic spirits* are not confined by material barriers to one limited space. Our spirits can co-mingle with other spirits, whether they be in the body or out of the body. *This is the fellowship of the spirit*. . . ."

"The modern disciple, taught by psychology, *focuses his attention upon Christ* in all the goodness of His character and all the power of His Spirit. Through the perfect Man he enters into communion with the infinite God. It is *a fellowship of the spirit*. . . ."

"Each human mind, while it is in a limited sense an individual mind, is at the same time a part of the universal mind. Each human spirit, while it has characteristics of its own, is at the same time a part of the universal spirit. . . ."

The peril of calling the psychical "spiritual" is strikingly shown in these quotations from current literature. Let us once more emphasize the difference between "soul" and "spirit" as revealed in the Scriptures.

The word "psychic" is derived from the Greek word *"psuche"* which is translated into English in the New Testament forty times as "life" or "lives" and fifty-eight times as "soul." It means, says the Lexicon, "animal life" or the "animal nature." It describes the "soul": the person when *animated by the life of nature.*

The "first man," made a "living soul," is clearly said to be "of the earth—earthy"; the "Second Man" was "the *Lord* from heaven" (1 Corinthians 15:47–48).

That the *"psuche"* nature is opposed to "spirit" comes out clearly again in 1 Corinthians 2:14, where it is written: "The natural [*psuchikos*] man rejects the teaching of God's Spirit, for to him it is folly, and he cannot comprehend it because it is *spiritually* discerned." This "psychical" man, says Conybeare in a footnote, is, "properly, man considered as endowed with the *anima* (the living principle) as distinguished from the *spiritual* principle." *"The animal man,"* he adds, would be the best translation, but the language is a little harsh in English.

"Psychic" power, therefore, which is so much to the fore today, is not "spirit," for it belongs entirely to man's *fallen nature.* The development of the "psychic faculty" is the

drawing out into action of some of the ca-
pabilities lying dormant in the "natural
man." The "forces" which are said by the
author of *Science of the Sacraments* to "ma-
terialize and accumulate within the very
body of the priest" are *natural* forces and
not from the Holy Spirit of God. They do
not constitute the "grace of God" as taught
in the Scriptures.

It is probably true that the psychic or
soul powers require supernatural power for
their full development, and that since the
Fall, this power is not of God but Satan. If
so, much that has been unaccountable in
the influx of satanic workings in the supernatural experiences of many of God's children during recent years becomes clear. It
also explains why a "baptism of power"
which was supposed to be of God could
result in the development of a "selfhood"
with *strong personal powers manifestly in
exercise*—instead of deep humility, broken-
ness of spirit, tender love of souls and ef-
facement of self.

Once again the Word of God gives the
answer to these fresh dangers of the day.
The cry on every side, reiterated even on
the pages of Christian magazines, is "Develop the personality." "Strengthen your
will." But what is the teaching of the Lord
Himself concerning the psychic or soulish
life? On the way to the cross, He bids those

who would follow Him to take up their cross and "lose" or "hate" their "psychic" (*psuche*) life, so as to save or keep it (the soul) to "life eternal." Once again the distinction between soul and spirit gives the key. As we have seen, the "soul" is either governed by the Spirit of God through the human spirit, thus drawing life from above (John 3:3, margin), or it is governed and animated by the animal life from the body—the lower realm—that is, *by the latent soul powers* drawn out into action and ofttimes mistaken for the *spiritual*. In the first case, governed by the Spirit of God, the man is a "*spiritual man*" and his "soul" is "saved"; in the second, the man is an "animal-soul" and his soul is lost. He that "loveth his life [*psuche*]," said the Lord, "shall lose it; and he that *hateth his life* [*psuche*] in this world shall keep it unto life [*zoe*] eternal" (John 12:24–25).

Does this not show that the "psychic" part of the life of nature is to be laid down and not "cultivated"? That the lower life of the *psuche* is, by the taking of the cross, perpetually to be kept out of action for the outworking of a higher kind of "life" from the Lord Himself, who is to His redeemed ones a "Life-giving Spirit."

How wonderful to see that the cross of Christ becomes to everything the "touchstone"! If "supernatural power" can draw into activity *psychic forces latent in the believer,* then it is not safe to accept any manifestation of "power" as of God unless it comes *by way of the cross* and leads the believer into the *path of the cross.* "Power" that results in the building up of "self," with *compulsory forces at work upon others,* simply means that *the psychic powers have been developed* instead of being kept latent and unused by the exercise of the cross. This alone makes way for the outflow of the Holy Spirit, who works upon the consciences of men not by forcing and compelling power but in conviction of the conscience by the light and truth of the Word of God.

6

THE DISTINCTION BETWEEN SOUL AND SPIRIT

FROM *FAUSSET'S COMMENTARY*

NOTE ON HEBREWS 4:12. "EVEN TO THE DIVIDING ASUNDER OF SOUL AND SPIRIT"— *i.e.,* reaching through even to the separation of the animal *soul (lower part of man's incorporeal nature, the seat of animal desires, which he has in common with the*

brutes; *cf. the same Greek,* 1 Corinthians
2:14, '*the natural [animal-souled] man,*'
Jude 19) from the *spirit (the higher part of
man,* receptive of the Spirit of God and
allying him to heavenly beings). "AND OF
THE JOINTS AND MARROW"—rather, (*reaching
even TO*) "*both* the joints [so as to divide
them] and marrow."

Christ "knows what is in man" (John 2:25):
so His Word reaches as far as to the most
intimate and accurate knowledge of man's
most hidden parts, feelings and thoughts, dividing, *i.e., distinguishing* what is *spiritual*
from what is *carnal* and *animal* in him, the
spirit from the *soul:* so Proverbs 20:27.

As the knife of the Levitical priest reached
to dividing parts as closely united as the
joints of the limbs and penetrated to the
innermost parts such as the *marrows* (the
Greek is *plural*), so the Word of God divides
the closely joined parts of man's immaterial being, soul and spirit, and penetrates
to the innermost parts of the spirit.

The clause (reaching even to) "*both* the
joints and marrow" is subordinate to the
clause "even to the dividing asunder of soul
and spirit." . . . An image (appropriate in
addressing Jews) from the literal dividing
of joints, and penetrating to, so as to open
out, the marrow, by the priest's knife, illus-
trating the previously mentioned spiritual
"dividing of soul and spirit," whereby each

(soul as well as spirit) is laid bare and "naked" before God; this view accords with v. 13.

Evidently "the dividing of the soul from the spirit" answers to the "joints" which the *sword, when it reaches* unto, *divides asunder,* as the "spirit" answers to the innermost "marrow." "Moses forms the soul, Christ the spirit. The soul draws with it the body; the spirit draws with it both soul and body." . . . The Word's dividing and far-penetrating power has both a punitive and a healing effect.

"DISCERNER OF THOUGHTS"—Greek, "*capable of judging the purposes,*" "INTENTS"—rather, "conceptions" [Crellius]; "ideas" [Alford]. As the Greek for "thoughts" refers to the *mind* and *feelings,* so that for "intents," or rather, "mental conceptions" refers to the *intellect.*

NOTE ON JUDE 19. "Sensual" (lit. "*animal-souled*") as opposed to the "*spiritual*" or "having the Spirit." It is translated "the natural man" in 1 Corinthians 2:14. In the three-fold division of man's being, body, soul and spirit, the due state in God's design is that "the spirit," which is the recipient of the Holy Spirit, uniting man to God, should be first and should rule the soul, which stands intermediate between the body and spirit; but in the . . . NATURAL man the spirit is sunk into subserviency to the animal-soul, which is *earthly* in its motives and aims. The "CARNAL" sink some-

spiritual   *natural*   *carnal*

what lower, for in these the *flesh*, the lowest element and corrupt side of man's bodily nature, reigns paramount.

"Not having the Spirit": In the animal and natural man *the "spirit*," his higher part, which ought to be the receiver of the Holy Spirit, is not so; therefore, his spirit not being in its normal state, he is said not to have the spirit. (*Cf.* John 3:5–6.)

NOTE ON 1 THESSALONIANS 5:23. "Spirit, soul and body . . . entire." It refers to man in his normal integrity, as originally designed. . . . All three, spirit, soul and body, each in its due place constitute man "entire." The "spirit" links man with the higher intelligences of heaven and is that highest part of man which is receptive of the quickening Holy Spirit (1 Corinthians 15:47). In the "unspiritual" the spirit is so sunk under the lower animal soul . . . that such are termed "animal" (English Version *sensual*, having merely the body of organized matter, and the soul the immaterial animating essence), having not the Spirit.

NOTE ON 1 CORINTHIANS 2:14. "Natural man": lit. *a man of animal soul*. As contrasted with the spiritual man, he is governed by the animal soul, which overbears his spirit, which latter is without the Spirit of God (Jude 19). So the animal (A.V. *natural*) body, or body led by the lower animal nature (including both the mere human,

fallen reason and heart), is contrasted with
the Spirit-quickened body (*cf.* 1 Corinthians
15:44–46). The carnal man (the man led by
the bodily appetites and also by a self-ex-
alting spirit, estranged from the divine life)
is closely akin: so too the "earthly." Devilish or   demon-like, led by an evil spirit
(James 3:15), is the awful character of such
a one in its worst type. . . .

NOTE ON 1 CORINTHIANS 2:15. *"He that is
spiritual,"* lit. "the spiritual (man)." In v. 14
it is "A [not *the* as in A.V.] natural man."
The spiritual is the man distinguished above
his fellow men as he in whom the Spirit
rules. In the unregenerate, the spirit which
ought to be the organ of the Holy Spirit
(and which is so in the regenerate) is over-
ridden by the animal-soul and is in abeyance,* so that such a one is never called
"spiritual."

NOTE ON 1 CORINTHIANS 3:1. "And I . . ."
i.e., as the natural (animal) man cannot
receive, *so I also could not speak* unto you
the deep things of God, as I would to the
spiritual; but I was compelled to speak to
you as . . . to "MEN OF FLESH. . . ."

The former (lit. *fleshly*) implies men
wholly of flesh, or natural. *Carnal* or
"fleshly" implies not that they were *wholly*

---

*Alas, too often the "animal-soul" overrides the spirit, even in
the regenerate.

natural or unregenerate but that they had much of a *carnal tendency, e.g.,* their divisions. Paul had to speak to them as he would to men *wholly* natural . . . not withstanding their conversion.

NOTE ON JAMES 3:15. "Sensual," lit. *animal-like*: the wisdom of the "natural" man . . . DEVILISH in its origin . . . and also in its character, which accords with its origin.

7

SOME SOULISH COUNTERFEITS OF SPIRITUAL REALITIES

E very genuine *spiritual* phenomenon has its *soulical* counterpart. For example, the love of truth, or *love viewed as a spiritual phenomenon,* differs essentially from the *soulical* counterfeit. Soulical love, as consisting in sentiment and the strong stirrings of affection, is a mere fleshly principle. It shuns suffering, it courts worldly enjoyment and consideration, it exhibits itself in the strength of the domestic and social attachments, and in its most refined form takes a deep interest in alleviating the miseries and promoting the comforts of the family of man. All this may exist with deep-rooted hatred to the truth.

Love as a divine principle and *spiritual*

phenomenon is distinguished by properties exactly the opposite of all this. It is love to God and is the result of our knowing that God has first loved us (1 John 4:19).

While *soulical love* pretends to cherish attachment to the Creator through the medium of the creature, *spiritual love* goes out to the creature through the medium of the Creator. *Soulical love* would, for the promotion of the apparent good of the creature, sacrifice at any time the truth of the Creator, whereas *spiritual love* rejoices to know that through the truth of the Creator the real good of the creature is secured and promoted.

Spiritual love is emphatically *attachment to the truth* and *attachment to others for the truth's sake.* Soulical love, though appearing to be spiritual, may be detected to be what it is by this test, that the truth of God is always in its estimation secondary, whereas the essential feature of spiritual love is its supreme and exclusive attachment to the truth of God.

The *soulical nature* of love professed often betrays itself in a great anxiety to reconcile the Word of God with well-established human facts and cogent human reasonings founded thereon, this even at the expense of God's veracity being compromised and encroached on. However, the language of *love which is divine and spiri-*

tual is, "Let God be true, though every man should prove to be a liar."

Selected.

Particulars of the magazine
The Overcomer
may be obtained from:

The Overcomer Literature Trust
9-11 Clothier Road
Brislington, Bristol
Avon, BS4 5RL, England.